COLOR, EBONY

COLOR, EBONY

by HELEN CALDWELL DAY

SHEED & WARD · NEW YORK · 1951

Author's Note

In order to prevent embarrassment, I have used fictitious names for some of my friends who appear in this book.

Acknowledgment

Most of the chapters in this book have previously appeared in *The Sun Herald*.

Contents

(*viii*)

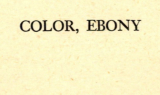

COLOR, EBONY

1. The Beginning of the Story

"How is it down South?"

"I guess you people have it pretty hard down there, don't you?"

Such questions as these are not too infrequent in a "mixed" sanitarium such as I was in, and even when they are not actually put into words, I have seen them in the eyes, and trembling on the lips, of a white patient too "well-bred" to ask them, or to ask, "What's it like, being a Negro?"

How strange it is that such a question should have significance in a Christian country. How strange that it should have so much significance that a great many friendly white people dare not ask it at all for fear of causing pain or giving offense; strange but indisputable.

How often have you wanted to ask your colored neighbor, co-worker or friend about the problems, the hurts or the needs peculiar to him as a Negro, and dared not, but remained in shamed silence, feeling the chasm between you a pain, and not knowing how to cross it?

This is going to be the story of a Man who did cross it, more than it is my story. He has shown us the way, but we have come a long way from Him, farther than we think.

In the sanitarium we often spoke of this, ten of us in our dormitory, five white, five Negro. And we also discussed those other two topics almost universally taboo in English-speaking countries in polite conversation— religion and politics. Now I think we are beginning to see, except those of us who deliberately blind ourselves to facts, that the three are inseparable, interdependent and of vital import in our daily lives, try as we may to exclude them from our conversations.

What we believe about God decides what we will think about other peoples and directs our actions in politics, business or any other element in our lives. What you think about God has determined my opportunities; what I think of Him has determined my use of the opportunities presented me.

You, my friends who love me, and you, who read this and do not know me and will never see me—what you call your own personal belief about God has influenced my life by deciding what outward circumstances surround me. Sometimes it's good to look back and see what we have made and are making of my life, you and I, according to the help God has given each of us within His Providence.

I am a Negro. Before I became ill, I was studying nursing at Cumberland hospital in Brooklyn and was in my senior year. I was born twenty-three years ago in Marshall, Texas, a town like hundreds of other small towns in the South except that it boasted two Negro colleges, Bishop and Wiley. My father taught music at Bishop and my mother taught in a kindergarten.

When I think of it, it seems very presumptuous for one so young to speak so surely of life, of eternal life at that, since youth is just beginning to live. And yet it was Our Lord who said, "I praise thee, Father, Lord of heaven and earth, that thou didst hide these things from the wise and prudent, and didst reveal them to little ones."

So I have dared to write of God and eternal things—though with "fear and trembling." I know that with God we are neither young nor old, wise nor foolish, black nor white, East nor West, but just souls, all needing His help, all created in His likeness to share His life.

But I know that with men we *are* black and white, rich and poor, wise and foolish—and this is also part of the story that I have tried to tell: what it is like, being a Negro, being poor and black in America today.

2. God Loves Everybody

WHEN WE WERE small children and going to grammar and high school, we moved many times from state to state, so most of our schooling was private. During those years my father alternately taught school, went to school to study, or worked as a pharmacist.

When he taught school, we joined whatever church was associated with the college at which he was teaching. Sometimes we were Methodists, sometimes Congregationalists. I never saw much difference in them, and apparently my parents didn't either, since they changed so readily. It didn't matter to me what church I went to, for I would believe as I liked anyway.

When I first started to school we were living in Iowa City, Iowa, and either I was too young to feel it (which is doubtful), or the people there were very unprejudiced indeed against Negroes, because I never felt the sting of color until we moved to Mississippi several years later. I knew that I was colored, but it was like knowing you have blond hair or black eyes—a fact, but not really important.

In Mississippi, the colored children my own age already knew what color meant; so they played among themselves, observing the rigid rules of color as meticulously as their parents. The white children didn't seem to know it as well; and when I tried to make friends with a pretty little blond girl who lived not far from me, she was willing enough. While we were playing one day, her mother saw us and came up angrily and carried her child off.

"What are you doing playing with that little Nigger?" she demanded of her.

"Go home to your mama and don't come back here any more," she ordered me threateningly. I ran home crying to my mother.

"Am I a Nigger?" I demanded in frightened tones. I had heard the term used. I knew that it meant something bad, something shameful. I knew that the very mention of it could make my self-controlled father and my gentle, even-tempered mother furious, and it had never occurred to me that the term could be used in regard to myself. My father looked at my mother. "Velma—" he began.

"I'll take care of it, Mr. Caldwell," she replied. (She always addressed him thus.) She tried to explain to me that I was a Negro and that "Nigger" was a term of insult to my people. She tried to make me feel her own pride in being a Negro. She is light-skinned, like an Italian or Spaniard, growing darker as she gets older, but unlike many light-skinned Negroes, she has none of the pride of color and the secret shame that makes it seem one is apologizing for being colored. She tried to make me feel as she felt, glad of what I am. But I was too hurt to understand or appreciate what she was saying about color.

"Does God love colored people? God is white." I wondered as I asked it.

"God is not white, nor any color. God is no color and every color and He loves everybody," my mother reassured me, and for a time my bitterness passed.

Sometimes it's hard, being a Negro. It's hard because it takes faith to teach "God loves everybody." And it takes faith to believe it.

(5)

3. Prayers and Tantrums

My MOTHER was the one who made God real to us, because He was real to her, although she was not what you would call a pious person. She attended church regularly and belonged to this and that organization; she taught us our prayers and sent us to Sunday school, but to her religion was an extremely personal thing, and it too should be "well-bred."

At home we had grace at meals; my father would " 'turn thanks," and the rest of us would repeat Bible verses, or sometimes little prayers of thanks. Such is the custom of most colored families in the parts of the South in which I lived. It has become a custom, a formality that often means as much as the conventional greeting, "How are you?"

We were never taught to love or really to try to understand the verses. Rather, it was an exciting game in which we each tried to outdo the other in finding odd or "catchy" verses. It was a sort of undeclared law that the same verse was not to be used too many times in succession by the same person.

My aunt "Big Helen," then a young girl, used to say all the time, "Lord, make us thankful for what we are about to receive." One day, as soon as she said it, my oldest brother, George, whom we called Junior, poured a pitcher of cold water on her. We all thought that it was hilariously funny at the time—so little did we understand the real significance of prayer and giving thanks. Repetition of the same prayer did not make us understand and love it more. Instead it caused boredom or annoyance.

Yet it was a good custom, because the finding of verses in the family Bible did lead to an interest in and love of the holy book.

Although we found repetition in our daily prayers monotonous and wearying, that was not true of our night prayers, which were always the same for my brothers and myself. My mother taught us, "Now I lay me down to sleep," but Junior learned another one in school which he taught me, and I always said it thereafter, because I liked it better:

> "Jesus, tender Shepherd, hear me.
> Bless thy little lamb tonight.
> Through the darkness near me
> Keep me safe till morning light."

Then came all the blessings: "Mommie and Daddy, Junior and William, Big Helen and Clara, Rex and Kitty and everybody, and make me a good little girl. Amen."

But although religious observances and teachings were part of our daily life, they were not a forceful, vital or informing part. Our parents wanted us to have a "normal, well-balanced life," and a bit of religion added a softening touch.

Other interests and traits, even pride and self-will, were encouraged much more. I had a perfectly vicious temper. Tantrums were not at all infrequent when my will was thwarted. And I was taught that I must practice self-control so that I might be successful and well-liked, not in order that I might please God. Thus our life was to be

(7)

ruled by reason, not by faith. However, I didn't particularly care whether I was liked or not and was convinced that I could have anything I really wanted in life, including success if I wanted it badly enough. So tantrums and willfulness continued. Reason was not strong enough to be for me a supreme guide.

We set this life and its happiness as our goal. Heaven, Hell, eternity, these were just words that didn't greatly concern us. And all the while the infant Christ struggled in our hearts for the birth we wouldn't give Him. And we never dreamed how limited reason is. I learned only by suffering to live by faith.

There were long long arguments or discussions, whichever you want to call them, at home between my brothers, Junior and William, my half-sister, Clara, and myself. Sometimes Big Helen joined in these also, but I don't remember her particularly in this connection. We all had our dreams, but the others only said they hoped theirs would come true. I said I knew mine would, and this always angered Clara, who was much older than I, and more experienced, since much of the time she was away from home, either studying or teaching. "Don't be so sure of yourself," she would say. "You are no different from the rest of us."

But I didn't like to believe that. I loved to think of myself as someone very special and set apart. Humility was a thing to be despised. "You can have anything in life you want, if you want it badly enough, if you are willing to pay the price for it," I would answer arrogantly. "At least, *I* can."

Many times this would lead to ridiculous arguments that lasted until Daddy, thoroughly disgusted at our pettiness, would say, "Oh, for God's sake let her alone and be quiet, or think of something else to argue about."

They would say, for instance, "Then tell me how you would get to be queen of England," or, "I'd like to see you boss Rock Island Railroad," or, "I'd like to see *you* as Mrs. Bilbo."

"I don't want to be any of those things," I would reply superciliously, "but if I did, I could. Everything has its price. If you are willing to give everything you've got for what you want, you can have it." And I would actually try to show them how I would go about getting the most impossible things. It was at this point that Daddy usually tired of the argument.

"You kids would argue with a stone wall if it could hear you," he might say. "Talk about something sensible, will you?"

"Little Helen's got a lot to learn, that's sure," Clara would mutter, undefeated.

"I bet *you* won't teach it to me, though," I would retort, rudely. "Ha!"

"Let her alone!" Daddy would say, defending me. "I am glad she feels like that. That's the spirit we need to get anywhere in this world. It's a pity a great many more of our people don't have it. If they did, maybe we could get somewhere."

Yes, I was proud, and there was plenty of food to nourish it always.

4. Faith of Our Fathers

My father attended church regularly because he often directed the choir or played the violin. Although he was a brilliant scholar in music, psychology and several of the natural sciences, he seemed to have little interest in religion, or even philosophy as such. He seemed to have little use for those things that his reason could not explain, or his mathematics calculate or his test tubes analyze.

Yet he was never a professed atheist nor agnostic. He observed the conventional religion of the "better-class" people around us. He was impatient with ignorance, superstition and anything that smacked of sentimentality or emotionalism. And I think he subconsciously identified all religious experience with one of the three.

Parents, of course, can't really *give* faith to their children. Only God can do that. But by cooperating with His grace within themselves and their children, they can spade and fertilize the soil in which faith is to be planted, and nourish the seedling which grows there.

Certainly, I am sure, my parents, especially my mother, tried to do this, but the missing, yet most needed, element was a greater certainty in their own faith. A good education, moderate financial and social security (despite the handicap of race), if possible the achievement of something "great" in one of the arts or sciences—such was the goal set before us.

Morality was important, and integrity, but morals could be separated from religion and God. God seemed to our unenlightened eyes more a force than a person. He was limited to a certain extent by His own laws of time and matter. Faith was a personal, private thing subordinated to education, independence and material security.

It is hard to make someone who is not a Negro, or who has not known real poverty or oppression, understand what those things mean to the Negro and to the very poor, and we were both. Under such conditions, these things assume an importance out of all proportion to everything else.

My parents were not materialists in the sense we most often use the word, nor was their ambition for us wholly selfish. It was an ambition and love for the whole race from which we have sprung. It was this consideration that kept my father in the poverty and ignorance of the South when other, more tempting jobs were available: love for my people.

Here are a people who have been brought from super-stition, ignorance and paganism into a "Christian" country and enslaved by its people. During and after the time of enslavement they were largely converted, not to Christianity, but to a mutation of it, which they themselves often distorted further by incorporating into it parts of their own pagan and superstitious doctrines and practices.

Their ignorance and lack of opportunity, plus the concept of free interpretation of the Scriptures, has produced many monstrosities of the faith to which they cling with the tenacity of a mother for her loved child whom she refuses to admit to be deformed and idiotic.

(*11*)

Here are a people who have suffered and cried to Heaven for a relief that seems long in coming. Like the prophet, "They looked and there was none to give aid." Like him, they can say, "I am a worm and no man," and "In peace is our bitterness most bitter."

So it is that God and religion have often been identified among them with ignorance and superstition, and these with oppression and slavery; while progress has been identified with a freedom from slavery and religion. In my home, during my childhood, the term "religious fervor" called to mind the frenzied moaning and shouting and dancing of some of the members of the small, unorthodox Protestant sects that grew up and thrived in Holly Springs and Memphis. It made us think of the heat and perspiration of human bodies in something like sensual abandonment as they "testified" to things even we children knew were not true:

"I thank the Lawd, children, that He kept me from sin, that I have not been drunk or gambled or run around with some other man's wife, but I am pure and sanctified!" Such testimony did not agree in any instance with what we knew of the man's private life. We talked about that at home, and we had our own ideas about religion.

"I think there is a God, but He is bigger than anything we can imagine about Him, so we just have to figure out our own way. He's through telling us how—if He ever did."

"I don't believe there is a Hell, though. No good God would permit that. I guess everybody does the best he knows how. Some people are just weak, I guess."

"I don't believe that. You are responsible for what you do, whether you like it or not."

"Oh, yeah? What about heredity and environment? Ever hear of those?"

"You know some sociologists claim that everything is due to environment."

"You probably mean psychologists. Some say heredity too."

"I don't care what they say!" (That would be me.) "I'll be what I want."

"Maybe you were born to."

"I don't know about that but I will."

"If God wills."

"Humph. I guess God doesn't care particularly, one way or the other. He's got Heaven to think about, never mind me."

Daddy never said anything in these arguments; but Mother might say, "You don't sound like a person who went to church and prayed no later than last Sunday. Remember, Christ hears you when you speak like that. He died for all of us."

That might sober us a moment, but it didn't change our ideas on religion or fervor. That was something for the ignorant, the stupid, the superstitious and the un-educated. It wasn't a part of us, nor did we want it to be.

But, apart from this, "religious fervor" called to mind a white man's disparaging remark, "Give a Nigger a woman, a bottle and a prayer book and you've got him." Thus, often-times the first thing a Negro gives up with success and education is the one thing no person should ever surrender—Faith.

5. The Forgotten Poor

When I was nine years old, we were really a part of the forgotten poor. We were living in Memphis, Tennessee. Daddy wasn't teaching that year. The year before he had taught at a college where bad students could be passed for monetary, social, or political considerations. Daddy never gave even his own children a better mark than we deserved, so he would not agree to that.

He had not gotten another position teaching yet, so he rented a cafe. Mother had to do most of the work there, however, because he went over to Arkansas to work on a farm.

The cafe was in the slums. In the same neighborhood were a place you could buy bootleg whiskey, and several "houses of pleasure." We used to see the women waiting on the street corner or sitting on their porches, smiling at men passing by and inviting them inside.

On Sunday they would dress up and go to nearby churches. During the week, sometimes the preacher or some of the elders would visit them, occasionally stopping off at our cafe to try to buy whiskey (which we did not sell).

We would think about that on Sundays at church when we saw them clapping, shouting and getting "happy." They would "testify" and tell you all about trusting and loving God, and about people going to Hell for playing cards and dancing, and seem to see no incongruity in what they said and the way they lived. Maybe that is one reason we didn't go to church very often then, and why mother didn't insist.

At home, Junior, William and I had our own household assignment and had to help in the cafe when it was very busy there.

Our friends were, for the most part, not too good for us, having already been corrupted by a depraved environment. We heard and saw many things children (or adults) needn't see or hear. In that neighborhood, God's name was a curse and sex an obscenity. Marriage was a dirty joke, and perversion something curiously fascinating.

Mother and Daddy tried, but could not shield us from all these things. Sometimes our neighbors invaded the very privacy of our home. One night a white prostitute came into the cafe, crying and drunkenly maudlin. Daddy wanted to put her out, yet dared not touch her because she was white. For our sakes he didn't want any trouble.

I didn't know and tried to comfort her. She hugged, kissed and flattered me, telling me her troubles.

"Mother, can't we help her?" I wanted to know. She said she was hungry. "Mother, feed her. See, the poor lady is hungry."

My mother listened, soothed and fed her, though she mostly took only coffee. Finally she went away, and I heard Mother and Daddy talking. Daddy said she had been taking dope. Mother said she wished we could move, because this was no place for children, and Daddy agreed.

There were too many things like that which they couldn't hide, and we were getting old enough to see and wonder about them. Then there were our play-mates. The children of the slums see and know about a lot of vice and corruption, and since we were a little backward, and behind on some of this knowledge, they lost no time in teaching us. There was no relationship that was not blasphemed:

"Hi kid, I saw your mama last night."

"Nigger, is you trying to put me in the dozen?"

"Not if your pappy aint." Then would come the fight. Anything about "mama" was fighting words.

Then there was poverty, as we knew it, itself. There was nothing glorious or beautiful about it. And I hated it. I hated wearing other people's cast-off clothes. I was not glad when people gave or offered me things that I needed. I was angry and ashamed that they should see my need. I wanted to hide it. It seemed to me that it was bad enough just being a Negro, without having to be poor as well. It was bad enough being dark without being dowdy.

One thing that might have made it harder was the fact that we continued going to private school long after we could afford it. It was a school made up for the most part of "upper-class" Negroes; that is, those in the pro-fessional fields, successful Negro businessmen and those light enough in color to "pass" for white. (The color caste system within the Negro race itself is the paradox of paradoxes. Here is the same group of people, on one hand decrying the injustice of white racial prejudice, fighting against "white supremacy" and racial segregation; and on the other hand, themselves erecting color barriers against those members of their race whose skin is a darker color than their own.)

There was one little girl in my class who I thought

looked just like Shirley Temple, then so popular—white-skinned, fair, with red-gold curls and blue eyes. Dressed like a doll always, she seemed to me to have all the things I wanted. She and girls like her would tell us of places they had gone to eat, or shows that they had seen, which were forbidden to the rest of us.

"Oh, I don't mind 'passing' for that. It's fun! 'Colored only!' "—she said it disdainfully— "I am as white as any of them."

Then someone who couldn't boast of color would boast instead of what she had or was going to get. "I wouldn't pass if I could. I am not ashamed of being colored. My mama says that when you've got something, it doesn't matter what color you are. We go North every summer, and then I can see all the shows I want to, wherever they are showing, and I don't have to lie about what I am; I don't have to pretend."

"Oh, yes, everything is better up there—the places, the clothes even."

"Umn humph. Especially the clothes. My mama gets all of mine up there. She has ordered my Easter dress already—white with little rose buds all around the yoke and a blue satin belt."

"I've already got my Easter outfit—pink satin and organdy with socks and hat to match, but blue shoes and bag. You should see them. What are you getting, Little Helen?"

"I don't know. We don't go in much for that sort of thing." (This said very superiorly, but hurting inside.)

"Mother says that your daddy hasn't got a job now. I bet you are too poor to buy anything."

"I'll have something all right; don't you worry about that."

"Oh, I'm not worried. *I* already have what I want. My daddy makes plenty of money."

"Yeah, I heard your daddy doesn't like Negroes any better than the next white man" someone else, perhaps an older girl, would say nastily.

"I guess you didn't hear that you' own was just a stool pigeon for Mr. Crump, 'licking white folks' boots to get ahead himself, and damn the rest of your people'— that's what my daddy says."

Someone would usually stop it before it went any further; it seldom came to blows.

All of it wasn't like this, of course; there were a few children there like myself, who were little and poor. They were timid though, and mostly kept quiet. There were others unspoiled by their color, social position or possessions. They were kind when they thought of you, and never cruel in this respect. Their parents would not have tolerated it for a moment, because they were good, and their philosophy Christian. It was this philosophy they wanted to give their children. Their friendship could disregard poverty. But mostly it was hard being poor.

6. Statistics

EVEN TO THOSE who do not believe in God, divorce statistics today are alarming. Our Lord does not need statistics to tell Him how important the family is. He established the family, and made marriage a sacrament, a means of obtaining God's help. He knew something that the bare written figures can never convey: all the fears, darkness, insecurity and human suffering that lie behind every statistic on record—for every figure represents a family. He knew all about the tears and bitterness that mark those most innocent. Not, of course, as He knows—but I too know.

When I was eleven years old, a new kind of trouble had come upon our family. We children were living in Holly Springs, Mississippi, with Daddy. Mother was still in Memphis. In the summer, and during some weekends and holidays, we lived with her. For a year now my parents had been separated, and they were considering divorce. We loved and wanted both our parents, and they both loved and wanted us. Hence our love and loyalty were divided. It seemed that whatever we gave to one was taken from the other, and we were mixed up, puzzled and miserably unhappy as only children can be. For children love so fully, so unreservedly.

I don't know what we had been taught about divorce. I know our Church permitted it. But certainly nothing could be right, I believed, that tore parents so violently from each other and their children, wounding everyone and making no one happy. We couldn't explain it to our friends, and we couldn't understand it ourselves:

"Helen, where is your mother?"

"She is in Memphis."

"Why doesn't she come to live here with you?"

"She is working over there."

"Mother says she and your daddy had a fight and she isn't coming to live with you any more."

"That isn't so! It isn't! It isn't!"

Then, later, with Mother: "Mother, why don't you come to live with us in Holly Springs?"

"I don't want to live in Mississippi, honey. There is no future for us there. It is too hard for a Negro. There are too many things you children want and need. You couldn't have them if we were there. Your Father is a brilliant man at his books, but there are so many things he can't understand. He wants to help others: that's all right. But you've got to think of your own family first. He can't see that. Try to understand."

And with Daddy: "Daddy, why doesn't Mother come to live with us?"

"She doesn't want to."

"Then why don't we go to live with her?"

"I think that is my business." Then later, as if sorry for his harshness: "There is a future here in Mississippi for those who are willing to work and wait for it. And the people here need me. There are a lot of possibilities here. Try to understand."

But I was sick of trying to understand. Never mind the people here; never mind the people there. Never mind the things even that they thought we wanted or needed. What about us—just us, ourselves?

I saw Clara, my half-sister, who was already a woman, in a new light now. She had been the child of my father by a previous marriage that had likewise ended in divorce. I had never understood her or loved her very much, because she had always been "difficult," unstable and maladjusted. Now I felt a new tenderness for her, as I began to understand a little of what her life had been like. I was wildly determined that the same thing should not happen to my brothers or to me. I thought I could prevent it some way.

As the months passed, we were all more and more miserable, and darkness seemed to be closing in on me. Often I wished I could die. Then, I thought, my parents would be sorry that they had made me so unhappy. Then they would go back together again, and my brothers would be happy. I couldn't die, though, by just wishing. But I could run away. Wouldn't that serve the same purpose?

A childish fancy? Perhaps every child has had such thoughts from time to time. But I was in dead earnest. The more I thought about it, the easier and more logical it seemed. I decided I would run away.

As the time which I had set drew near, I was afraid but still determined. I turned more and more to God for comfort and courage. I learned to talk to Him in prayer that was like conversation. But like John in C. S. Lewis' *Pilgrim's Regress*, I was not certain to Whom or even What I prayed, even while I was certain that He would help me. My attitude was, "He to Whom I pray knows to Whom I pray."

7. Round Trip to Jonesboro

ALMOST ANOTHER YEAR passed before I ran away. It was early in October when I decided "Next week is it. Next week I'm going to run away." I was almost twelve and in the ninth grade. I continued going to school and studying my lessons as if nothing were wrong or unusual.

As the day drew near, I lost most of my fears. I felt sorry for the pain I would cause those who loved me and which I would suffer myself, but I thought all our eventual happiness was worth it. I really believed that this act would make my parents forget about divorce and come back together again.

Often I was lonely. Then I used to ask my grandmother, my mother's mother, to guard and protect and comfort my mother, since she would no longer have a daughter nor I a mother. Whenever we had visited Grandma in the past she had been very good to me; now I prayed to her as to a saint, for she was dead.

I don't know what made me do that. Certainly it was not something I had gotten from the faith I had been taught, because it denied the power of the souls of the living and the dead to intercede for or otherwise help each other, and considered death annihilation until the final resurrection of the dead at the Judgment. I only knew that, alive, she had loved me, and believed that somehow she must still be able to love, hear and help me.

The day before I was to go, I went down to the train station with my best friend, Celestine. A girl about my own age, Celestine shared all my secrets and knew of my plans. We picked Jonesboro, Arkansas, because the name appealed to us and it was about as far as my money would take me. She promised not to tell anyone (and never did, even when questioned by my parents, her mother and father, or by the officials of the juvenile court). I bought my ticket with money I had saved, and we went back home. Junior had a little money saved too, and I intended to help myself to that to pay for incidental expenses until I could find a job. I knew that it was stealing, but I justified it to myself on the grounds that I was doing it as much for his benefit as for my own.

The next day, early in the morning, I caught the train for Jonesboro. I had no difficulty. In Memphis I was strongly tempted to go to see or call my mother, but I did not. I passed through without making myself known.

On the train I thought of the letter I had left with the minister to be delivered to my father if I did not call for it on a certain day. It was a letter to both my parents, giving the proposed divorce as my reason for running away. I condemned it as wrong and unfair to us, and begged them to reconsider for our sakes and try to reconstruct their broken marriage. I said that if they did do this, I might return, because I would know. I also told them that if they tried to find me, I would run away again and again, as often as they found me.

Once in Jonesboro, I started looking for work and for a place to live. The first people I approached saw I was only a child and called a social worker. She questioned me, and I told her my name was Peggy Ann Darling, that I had recently lost my mother and had run away from the people who had been keeping me down in Mississippi because they wanted to make a harlot of me. I refused to tell the name of the place or the people, because I said I was afraid she would send me back and I would be forced into a kind of life my mother had taught me was wrong.

I don't know whether she believed me or not, but she placed me with a very nice Christian family, Mr. and Mrs. Smith Hubbard. They took me in and cared for me, just as if I were their own daughter, even letting me use their name. They took me to school and to church and to their friends' homes. Here they made it clear that whoever would not accept me need no longer accept them either.

So I became Peggy Ann Hubbard. I made friends, especially with two boys, the minister's son, Bernard, and a ball player in my high school, Alex. Bernard became my confidant, but I thought I loved Alex. I thought I'd like to marry him when I grew up. Of course, we never went anywhere together, we were both only children, but we wrote each other notes in school, and each of us giggled when the other passed.

I was often over to Bernard's house though, with my adopted parents, because they were his parents' friends. We talked about what we wanted to do when we grew up. I said I wanted to write. He wanted to be a minister like his father. We talked about God, and listened to his father when he talked or preached, and I think I believed in God then, in His mercy, love and justice. I don't know what happened to that faith later.

I remained with the Hubbards two months and then

returned to Memphis. I left them partly because my constant deception began to weigh on my conscience, partly because I was homesick.

When I returned to Memphis, and later to Holly Springs, I was welcomed and forgiven by the whole family. It became a closed incident, except that we never forgot the wonderful charity of those two people.

8. House Divided

When i had come back from Jonesboro, Mother in Memphis and Daddy in Holly Springs, each tried to make a home where we could grow into normal, healthy, well-adjusted adults. I think they convinced the judge of the juvenile court in Memphis that they could succeed in this, because each continued to have equal custody of us. I didn't even have to see Judge Kelly, but it was left to my parents to punish, correct and discipline me as they saw fit. I think, however, that gentleness and understanding were recommended.

Both parents wanted to make home so attractive that none of us would ever want to run away again. But what we could not decide was: which house was home? Mother's? Daddy's? Each blamed the other for what had happened. Within our hearing and to our knowledge, they had never quarreled or fought; so we had no way of knowing, of judging, who was right and who was wrong. We thought both were wrong.

The holidays, especially Christmas and Easter, were most difficult. Mother wanted us; Daddy did too. Either would have been hurt and disappointed if we failed to spend this special day at "home." But we could not cut ourselves in two. We could not be two places at once. The best we could do was spend the morning in one place and the evening at the other. Fortunately, it is only a two-hour trip between Memphis and Holly Springs.

One Christmas we had spent the morning in Memphis with Mother because she complained she never had us all together Christmas morning. She was so happy. There was a big tree and lights and a crib. There were the presents we had wanted and the joyous sounds of laughter and song.

"It's so good to have you here," she said. "Mother misses her babies when they're away."

We were happy too. Still, even in our happiness, we could not help remembering Daddy alone in Holly Springs in a silent house where the gaudy Christmas tree must only have intensified his loneliness. I kept remembering that he would have no Christmas dinner except what he might prepare for himself. I could imagine only too well how little heart he would have in fixing it.

Then there were our friends. Because we were in Holly Springs most of the year, most of our friends were there, those friends with whom we most liked to share our joys, sorrows and secrets. There was Celestine, for instance. We usually went to church together Christmas morning for the sunrise service, then went home and opened our presents together. Junior and William had friends like that too, and we missed their companionship this day. Yet we knew if we had been in Holly Springs, we would have felt guilty at our happiness with them when Mother was alone and missing us. So there seemed no really happy solution.

At three o'clock or thereabouts, we left for Holly Springs to spend the rest of the day with Daddy. It was almost dark when we arrived, and the house looked empty and lonely in the dusk, and seemed too silent.

Daddy's face was drawn and strange, and there seemed to be reproach in his greeting:

"Christmas didn't seem like Christmas somehow without you young folks around. I try to be daddy and mother to you, but sometimes I get discouraged."

That was the kind of holiday we all knew.

9. The Poor and Black

WE WERE ALMOST always poor, and our poverty was not that of the movies and drug store novels, nor even the comfortable "poverty" of the lower middle class, but the very real "pinch penny" poverty of those who know what it is to be hungry and have no food, who have to worry and wonder about the next pair of shoes or a coat for winter.

Some of the times were worse than others. Some of the times I was even too young to realize that we were poor. I just knew that when Daddy went to school, Mother had to work, doing domestic work for white families, washing, cooking, housecleaning. Sometimes she brought us food from their kitchens, or clothes or broken toys which they no longer needed or wanted for their own children.

I have a letter from my mother which she sent to me on my twentieth birthday. Each page tells what happened on my birthday—for twenty years.

On December 3, 1931, she says: "It's quite different this year. I am the only one working now. Dad is in school . . . We have only one big room . . ." (serving as bedroom, kitchen and parlor for mother, father and three children). "I pray God each night that you will be spared my heartaches . . . that you will never cry in the night as I have cried . . . You are too young to see or know . . ."

One year on my birthday there was not even enough money to buy the ingredients for the usual cake. But mother was undaunted. From neighbors and other faculty wives at the little college where my father received less than a laborer's salary, she obtained butter, milk, sugar and eggs. Even now, when I see milk and eggs wasted, I remember those days. Fresh, whole milk and eggs were luxuries to us. Eggs were used for cooking only, and canned milk took the place of fresh milk because it was cheaper, and easier to keep without ice.

When I became old enough to notice things, at first I hated being poor. I hated wearing hand-me-down clothes, and eating food from other people's kitchens. I was angry that my parents wouldn't "put on a front" and "keep up with the Joneses." It wasn't until years later that I began to understand, and adopted my father's philosophy: "that it is more important to be than to seem; only those who refuse to imitate are imitated." To me in my childhood, poverty was something of a disgrace, because people spoke of the poor with contempt. Charity was a shameful thing; to accept it was a mark of failure, disgrace.

What a paradox our lives were! As a college professor, my father was considered one of the "elite" by Negro standards, which base social distinction on profession or color. The professional people and those light enough to "pass" are the "cream" of society. (I am excluding wealth as a factor of distinction because outside of the professional classes, there are very few Negroes whose incomes reach beyond—or as far as—the income of the "middle class" white person. "Big business" is practically nonexistent. So is the caste of blood, except in New Orleans and a few other very old and wealthy towns of the South, and there it exists mostly among those of Creole descent.

Not long ago, a person who had been born in the South, but who had left it in early childhood, told me that the lives of the professional class of Negroes were greatly different from those of the ordinary Negro farmer or laborer, that the members of the professions were less subject to discrimination, and thus less affected by racial hatred and prejudice. Sometimes, and in certain circumstances, that may be true, but I disagree that it is the general rule. I know that it was not true of us.

Prejudice of that kind being an illogical thing, anything can happen, but where it exists, I have not found that money, prestige, intelligence, education, ability, or anything else the Negro can offer, greatly changes the situation in his favor. The hotels, restaurants, theaters, etc., which are closed to the most dirty, ignorant and unkempt colored person are closed also to the immaculate scientist; the church that is closed to the drunken brown harlot is closed also to the visiting colored minister of the same denomination. "White only" means just that, no matter who you are.

As a matter of fact, I have often found that among the most prejudiced of white groups in the South, the dirty, the ignorant, the disreputable Negro gets the best breaks. This extends even to the criminal Negro, as long as his crime has been directed against his own race—except in the case of theft (and even that is often tolerated from him). The superior Negro arouses jealousy and spiteful actions. He seems a potential threat, one who has forgotten "his place." Only the education, the religious training, the type of job opportunity that will keep the Negro in "his place" is encouraged. For that reason, the

(*31*)

"upper class" Negro frequently has to suffer not less, but more, from racial prejudice because of his color. He has to be reminded that "these things you have acquired, or these things you have learned, or this natural talent or ability you have, has not changed things: you are still a Negro. And a Nigger is a Nigger." One doesn't have to remind that poor black tenant farmer who lives on his farm with seven or eight children to stay in "his place." It is very unlikely that he will ever be able to leave it, even if he wanted to do so. But you are different. You might easily forget, so you must be reminded.

When Daddy had to go to town for groceries, or something like that, most clerks in the stores called him "Doc" or "Professor," or simply "Caldwell." But a few went out of their way to make an opportunity to address him as "Boy" or "Uncle." When that happened, he tried to avoid those stores in the future if it were at all possible— which sometimes it was not—or to avoid those clerks— which usually he could very easily do. His children got used to hearing themselves addressed, however, as "Boy" or "Girl"—as much as you ever get used to such things. We were not old enough to rate the more respectful title "Aunt" or "Uncle."

One of the Negro teachers there did find a way to stop this form of address to a large extent in one store, but her method could only have been employed by a woman.

As she went into a store one day, a bright young clerk walked up to her and asked her, kindly, "What will you have, Auntie?"

Our friend was warm in her response. She threw both arms around the clerk's neck in apparent affection. "Oh, my dear child!" she exclaimed sweetly, "I am so very glad to see you working here. Which one of my sisters' children are you?"

The clerk turned very red in her embarrassment, and those standing by, white and colored alike, laughed; they couldn't help it. She did look funny, and there was no question that she had brought it on herself.

After that, the clerks in this store didn't say "Auntie" or "Girl" or "Boy" so readily; usually it was, "What will you have, *Customer?*"

In traveling, in riding on buses or trains or merely stopping in the stations' Jim Crow waiting rooms; in going to the theaters, in seeking medical help or hospital or clinic care; in going to school or to church or looking for a house or room to rent; law, custom and tradition had countless ways of reminding us that we were no exceptions to the rule of color; we also were Negroes and must carry the dark man's burden.

So in one sense, we were the elite. But at the same time, we were poor, even by the Negro standard. And our friends were from the people. And we were colored, a part of the "inferior" race.

10. Small Town

Usually neither my father's nor our own intimate friends were to be found among the Negro "elite," the ministers, teachers, "successful" business people and their families. A farmer who cultivated a few acres of land ten miles from town to support a wife and seven or eight children; a comedian from a minstrel show with whom my father had once worked to earn money for school; a Pullman porter whom he had met in like manner, while working as a dining car porter; students from the school, restless, idealistic, not content with the complacency of the world as it is, but longing to change it to what it could be—ought to be: these were my father's friends, and ours were their young counterparts.

After we had moved to Mississippi the second time, we rented a house to ourselves. Mother wasn't with us then, but remained in Memphis, and I kept house. (It was during this time that our parents' separation issued in divorce.) In the winter we couldn't afford a fire all over the house—coal and wood were so expensive—so we usually kept one in the kitchen, one in my father's room and one in Junior and William's room. If I had company, I made one in my own room; otherwise, I stayed with my father or brothers or in the kitchen.

We sat around the stove, talking, arguing, wondering about the meaning and purpose of life, stating our ambitions, discussing the news of the day or whatever had caught our interest. Sometimes we played cards or games. Sometimes we had music—Daddy on the violin or trombone, Junior with a trumpet, and I with a melophone. William just listened. Those times were peaceful, happy and contented.

Other times were not. The small town tore us with its gossip. St. Francis says "detraction is a kind of murder." If it is, then we were murdered daily. I got the gossip sometimes first-hand and sometimes through my friend Celestine or her mother.

"Helen, you know, some folks are saying your mother and daddy were divorced about another man over in Memphis," Celestine would say.

Or William might come home and say, "Little Helen, I had a fight today with a boy at school, because he said something bad about you. He says his mother said you ran off to Jonesboro because you were going to have a baby—that everybody knows it. I said that it was a dirty lie and smashed him one. No one can say that about my sister." William was always so gentle and even-tempered, like mother, that this was something extraordinary from him.

Or a good friend like Henrine or Ollie Bell or Avery, who went with me to school, would say to me shamefacedly, averting her eyes, fidgeting, "You know I'd like to come to your house and visit you sometimes. It's not fair to make you come to see me all the time—but my mother—well, you know how people talk, all those boys around all the time, and no woman in the house. Of course, I know you wouldn't do anything wrong and I wouldn't either, and that they're Junior's friends and all, but it doesn't look right, my mother says. You come to see me. Or maybe I can stop a few minutes from school or church, Sunday, and mother won't have to know. Somebody might tell her though, but I don't guess she'd mind that."

Sometimes I'd tell Junior or his friends, and cry. Then they would comfort me and say, "The first one I hear say something like that about you is going to get his nose busted, nasty minded . . ."

Sometimes Celestine and I would talk about it: "You know, Celestine, some day it won't be like this. I'm going to be rich and famous; then I'm going to come back and make all of them eat every word they ever said about me or my mother. I'm going to snub everyone who ever snubbed me, and make them pay. I'm going to have something they all want, and I'm going to laugh at them for wanting it. They will be glad to say then that they went to school with me or lived next door!"

"You know, you scare me a little," she would say seriously, "when you talk like that. You are so sure of yourself. You believe it so much yourself, you make other people believe it. You are not like other people. But I believe you can do it. I guess you wouldn't have anything to do with me then."

And I would hug her: "Oh, not you, Sister. You will always be my friend, and your mother. You aren't like the other people around here. You are different. No matter what happens, we will always be friends."

And she would return my embrace: "Yes, no matter what happens, let's always be friends."

But the town went on talking, about me, about my mother, about my sister, about my father. We were

(36)

strange; our ideas were strange—unlike those of others around us in the way we regarded ourselves, white people and Negroes. Besides, we kept to ourselves and didn't talk much of the trifles and pettiness that made up small town gossip. But here was this divorce, something one could put her tongue to, and the unconventional way we lived—a very busy father and a house full of boys, always with only one small girl among them. Professor Caldwell needed a woman in the house —that was the consensus of opinion. And there was more than one woman who saw herself as ideal for the position. Daddy didn't seem to see them, though, so they talked and talked.

That kind of thing went on from the time I was eleven until I went to nursing school at eighteen. Seven years. Seven years is a long time when you are young, and spiritual wounds cut deep. The wounds are all healed now, but the scars are still there.

11. The Sound of Laughter

In the warm evenings from spring to fall there was the same friendly comradeship and understanding between us. There was always more company—Junior's or William's friends, who filled the house with the noise of their band practice, and with talk and laughter.

Sometimes their talk would be "boys' talk," and they wouldn't want me there. Then I would go for a walk in the country, taking the dog with me for protection and company. I liked to walk in the silence of evening and watch the sunset disappear and the dusk grow deeper until, in the darkness, stars appeared.

I liked the lonely sound of a dog's cry, the soft rustle of the wind through the tree branches. I liked the warm, sweet smell of the dust when dew had fallen in the summer. I wondered at the mystery of the heavens and what lay beyond the heavens, if It were God. It was the only time I felt really close to Him, then.

Most often, however, I joined the happy group in the boys' room. When we didn't feel serious we told tall tales or ghost stories, or sometimes sang or played music together. Most often, though, we spoke of race, or prejudice, or maybe of when we grew up, what we'd do to change things. We spoke of all the things we saw around us, what we heard, or read about the destitution, squalor, superstition and abysmal depths of ignorance in which most of our people are forced to live in the South. We spoke of towns where a Negro cannot live in peace and retain his dignity as a man, yet dares not leave except in secrecy, as a fugitive, by night. We spoke of the very real but disguised Negro slavery labeled "tenant farming," which still exists in many parts of the South.

Sometimes we spoke with bitterness, sometimes we spoke matter-of-factly, so much has suffering become commonplace and sorrow part of our heritage. Sometimes we even spoke with laughter. Laughter drowns out the sound of grief, and one must laugh at times to keep from crying.

One summer my father had barely escaped from such a farm in Arkansas; and he used to tell us stories to illustrate the Negro's status there. He was trying to show us how nearly impossible it was for a man to change his status even if he wanted to and tried; he just couldn't save enough money to make the break. I remember one in particular we often repeated.

At this particular farm there was one tenant who, being ignorant himself, wanted better opportunities for his children. So by almost starving himself (and them), he managed to put away a little money for their education every month out of his meager income.

But at the end of the year he had to go to the farm store, where all tenants must trade, and settle accounts with the farmer or his representative.

"John," the red-faced man behind the counter began calmly, "there was the sack of flour you bought—four dollars."

"Yes, suh." (Very agreeably.)

"And the one you didn't get." (Decisively.)

"Suh?"

(39)

"Shut up, nigger. Don't you know better'n argue with a white man?"

"Yes, suh."

"Four dollars. And the one you oughta got. Four dollars. That will be sixteen dollars for flour. Understand?" (Mockingly belligerent.)

"Yes, suh." (Resigned. Empty of hope. Despairing.)

We laughed when we repeated the story. And we told other stories like it.

"You know, they tell me that down near the Delta there's a town that's got written over the city gates, 'Nigger read and run, and if you can't read, run anyhow.'"

"That's like that sign in Memphis: 'No Negroes, peddlers or dogs allowed.'"

"I guess peddlers must be awfully mad, if they are white, when they see themselves classed with us and dogs."

"Yeah, maybe more for us than for the dogs! Ha!"

"Well, one sure thing, I'd rather be classed with a dog than with a lot of them I know."

"I heard a guy at the bus station the other day talking about a place down in Alabama where a Negro can't go out on the streets after dark except in his own neighborhood."

"I reckon they think they'll bite. Watch out, Mr. Tucker, old boy. Here I come, and I'm hungry! Grrr."

And we laughed again. But inside, pain kindled the fires of spirits into resolutions to change things and bring freedom and justice to dark men who had long since lost all hope of either, who had slept with despair until nature forced a marriage. Then we felt most keenly the stigma of being black and destitute.

12. Classroom of the World

My formal education was for the most part directed toward worldliness, success, progress—and I think you will agree that I am not alone. It was intended primarily to enable me to cope with a hostile world and to rise in it as far as my natural abilities would take me, despite the handicap of color.

To prepare us for a successful life in the world only, our school was intended to make us good citizens, responsible, respectable, self-supporting, a credit to our communities. Like a great many other religiously endowed schools (ours was supported by the Methodist Conference) the college and high school had God in its curriculum, but not in its spirit. French, Spanish, music, the arts, chemistry, mathematics, social sciences—these things were emphasized, these one had to learn as they were taught. But religion was left largely up to us.

There was a compulsory course in Bible Study, but it was very broad, and by the time we had read several contradictory commentaries, and heard the professors' lectures differing from all of them, we were pretty confused. We had some arguments and discussions of particular points of Methodist theology as we learned it, but they got nowhere, since each could prove by an "authority" that he or she was right. Others thought we were "bright" because we could do this.

(41)

In the social sciences such as history and civics we had to study from textbooks written by Southern white people for Southern white people. Here Negro slavery, segregation, Jim Crow, all these were shown in a favorable light, where possible were not only justified but shown as necessary. The Negro was shown as an inferior —ignorant, undisciplined, irresponsible, full of malice, or like a child. The text made a difference between "citizens" and "Negroes": "citizens' rights" meant "white rights" not "Negro rights."

Thus were Negro children conditioned to accept their inferior status, to look down upon their own race, and despair of their possibilities. To counter the bad effects of those textbooks, we were also taught Negro history. In the other class some teachers, whom we called "Uncle Toms," taught the textbooks as they were written, in the spirit of the author; others, more radical or less intimidated, taught the facts of the text in their own spirit, showing Negro slavery, segregation, Jim Crow, and the problems they created as the evils which they are. Of these, some said we must see these things in their true light but be patient and fight them indirectly by raising ourselves and others of our people to the fullness of the dignity proper to man, by education, by progress in business and civic responsibilities. Most of them urged us to prove ourselves worthy of citizenship's rights, that we might soon obtain them.

But this idea was based on the false notion that the primary reason a Negro is denied certain rights is because he is "not ready." It assumes that as soon as he is "ready" he will receive them. As a matter of fact, he would be considered "ready" by most people who put forth this argument to justify the racial injustice of the

South, about the same time the communists achieve their "classless society." And I don't think any one of us would like to wait in Hell till then.

Fortunately for me, my father was my principal teacher both at home and at school, and he does not have a mind that is easily intimidated. He was not content that we, nor any of his students, should learn merely subjects, but we were expected to learn to think logically and choose wisely and freely. In his classes or at home, a wrong answer with good reasoning behind it was more acceptable than a right answer given parrot-fashion, mechanically. He made the correction, showing where the reasoning went wrong by some false premise, and was pleased at the effort.

At home he liked us to have and show strength of will and purpose, even as he directed them to more acceptable channels. He kindled our love for knowledge from his own rich store, to nourish bodies and minds until we were able to stand alone and unafraid before other men.

"Never be ashamed of your race," he would say. "You have a great heritage. Live up to it, and be proud. When others see your self-respect they must respect you. Learn what your people have done and you will have no reason to be ashamed. Langston Hughes, Booker T. Washington, Countee Cullen, George Washington Carver—men like these have paved the way for you. You must pave the way for others; that is where greatness lies. Do you understand that?"

We understood, and we agreed. We learned Negro History at school in addition to our regular American or European or ancient history, and we studied at home the works of Negro writers and artists and musicians. I liked Countee Cullen especially because his work was sad and lonely, and at the same time arrogant and undefeated like my own spirit. He said so well the things I thought and felt and had not yet learned to put into words which would reach other people. I especially liked his *Shroud of Color* and *A Pagan's Prayer*. Both showed the Negro reaching out and failing and falling, and in his despair, denying God, his Creator, and reaching out again only in hope, finding God only if he found himself.

It's queer, how readily we forget, though, that we are soul as well as body and mind.

13. "A Negro Hasn't Got a Chance!"

"A NEGRO HASN'T got a chance." What a horrible, bald statement, but how close to being an ugly truth. I have heard it all my life, but it only angers me or hurts me from the lips of another Negro. Then it has in it an element of defeatism that too often presages despair, and with it the loss of hope and faith in God and in other men. It is the beginning of the end, a sort of preliminary echo to the torments of Hell.

A few years after the divorce, my mother remarried, and countless times during my adolescence I heard the above expressed from the lips of my stepfather, Don. Don was so different from my father. Daddy has a great love for and faith in people, especially the Negro people, and has dedicated his life and talents to teaching them and preparing them to be better and stronger people. But Don has let the experience of being a Negro embitter him somewhat against both races. He really believes that, generally speaking, the Negro is inferior, and he hates himself for believing it and being one himself. Daddy believes in a general sort of way in God, and in Christ as the messenger if not the son of God. Don believes the whole thing (Christian religion) is a hoax played by the Jewish people to keep the rest of the world subdued. He is kind and generous, but only to those he loves or those desperately in need.

(45)

Even more than our parents, he wanted us to turn out "big" or "great," to prove to the world and to him that color was not the determining factor in the greatness of a man. Yet he always discouraged us when we spoke of doing great things, because he thought we would be hurt by too great an ambition, which a Negro could never fulfill. He discouraged, yet all the while could not conceal his hope that we would not be discouraged, and he helped us to do or learn the very things he laughed or poked fun at when we spoke of them.

He especially poked fun at, ridiculed or spoke bitterly against religion, particularly Protestantism. He said it was one of the greatest forces for keeping the Negro in ignorance, superstition and destitution, and content with himself. He considered preachers the robbers and liars who preached fantasy. "As long as you listen to that, you don't have a chance," he insisted. "People get so worked up about some dreamed-up heavenly kingdom they forget about earth. I want my justice right here if there's a just God: don't give it to me after I'm dead. I don't need it then. Now is the time."

Mother could stand up to him and hold her own, her faith was that strong. My own was not so firmly grounded, and as my respect and admiration for him grew, so did my faith waver. I was ashamed to confess that I half-believed in Christ as God and in an absolute standard of good and bad. I was ashamed to confess that I half believed in Our Lord's death and resurrection. And by the time I reached my sophomore year in college, my ideas of God and his laws were very vague indeed, and I had discarded the idea of absolute standards of good and bad for a philosophy of "Anything I believe is right, is right for me, anything I believe is wrong, is wrong for me."

Thus with an unbelieving stepfather, and a half-believing father, both loved and admired, perhaps I would have finally given up my meager faith, except for my mother's influence and the unrecognized help of God. Instead, I compromised my faith more and more, and tried to "sit on the fence" of half-belief, not realizing that half-belief is none at all.

14. War

FROM ABOUT 1939 the war took precedence as a topic of conversation in our home. There were so many things to think about, to talk about, even before we actually entered the war. Junior, then in college, was of "draft age," and we were afraid that he would be called before he finished. There were rumors of the government taking over either Rust or Mississippi Industrial (another Negro college in Holly Springs), and we wondered what would happen to the students and teachers. And always there was the question "What will the war mean to the Negro? What will be his place in it? What about afterwards?"

None of us were very optimistic. Those of us who were too young to remember 1914 had heard enough about the first war to alarm us. Would the Negro take the responsibilities of a citizen once more, only to be denied the rights of a citizen again when it was all over? A lot of colored people were already saying, "This is a white man's country, let him fight for it! White folks always say this is their country; they can have it now. Let them die for it." Aloud, we said, "It's our country, too." Yet there were times when we, also, doubted.

On one side there were the Negro weekly newspapers with their headlines, "Negro G.I. Blinded by White Police Officer Following Dispute with Bus Driver"; "Race

Riot in Detroit Continues with Unabated Violence";
"Negroes Denied Union Membership in Deep South"—
always headlines giving evidence of increased racial ten-
sions ending in violence, so many injured, so many dead.

On the other side were the regular dailies and their
headlines condemning the Nazi denial of human rights to
the Germans and the conquered peoples who opposed
the regime.

We all knew with reasonable certainty that we would
finally enter the war, we would eventually be asked to
contribute our share to the hate and violence of the sick
world—and for what?

That was the question we could not answer satis-
factorily, the question that tortured. We were afraid of
the answer. If there is some fine distinction between the
persecution of the Jews by the Germans and the persecution of the Negro Americans by the white Americans,
we could not see it. So in our hearts love and loyalty
for our country warred with distrust and suspicion of
our fellow countrymen.

We did not see the war as an evil in itself, but only as
a futile, bitter struggle that neither side won, and which
most hurt those most innocent on each side. The Christian
ideal of peace for the sake of love had no real influence
on our hatred of war, but it was the experience of seeing
the terrible fruits of hate in our own or others' lives.

Even a little town like Holly Springs showed the touch-
iness of a war-conditioned people. Negro-White relations were usually quiet, if not peaceful; racial resentment
hid itself under Southern courtesy and custom. Now we
were getting away from that. Walking down the street,
two white men deliberately ran into and shoved me.
Junior and his friends, Haynes and "Buttercup," wanted

to beat them up and shoot them. Daddy and I had to quiet them.

"No white So-and-so is going to run over *my* sister and get away with it! Where does he come off? Stinking peckerwood! I'll fix him so he can't walk if he won't look where he is going."

"Now, Son—"

"Look, Pop, if you had been there you would feel the same way. I know you. Didn't you always tell us to stand up for our rights? No, I'm going to kill him! If it had been *his* sister, he'd have had a whole mob by now. He even cursed her. But if I look—so much as just look —hard at a white girl, they are all ready to scream 'Lynch the Damn Nigger!'

"I'm good enough to do their dirty work. I'm good enough to fight in their damn army if they call me, and we all know they probably will. I'm good enough to pay taxes if I own anything. But when it comes to ordinary human rights, I am not good enough for them. When it comes to ordinary human respect, I am not good enough for that. They won't give me any rights, so I'll take them; they won't give me any protection under the law, so I'll protect myself and my sisters. No white man shall touch them disrespectfully and live to boast about it!"

We talked and talked to him. After a while the others were quiet. Junior was quiet too, but unconvinced. A white friend, Mr. Smith, talked to him too, and to the other men, the white men. "That's a nice kid," he told them. "He doesn't bother nobody. He don't pick no fights. But he's mad now, and that's the kind of guy that will get mad and kill you. I'm a white man and you are a white man. But the kid is in the right this time, and I'll stand behind him. You don't live here, and you are trying to make trouble for those of us who do. The best thing you can do is get out of town, back where you belong. That Caldwell kid will kill you."

Finally, between us, we calmed them all down, even Junior. We heard nothing further from the two men, although they were angry at Mr. Smith, calling him a "Nigger lover." I suppose they took his advice, though, and left, because we never heard anything more from them nor saw them again.

But there were other things to remind us always that we were colored, and what that meant. Negroes waiting for tickets in the bus stations were treated rudely and contemptuously by the whites, who seemed to believe that war and the fact of being a fighting man was making the Negro forget his "place." One Negro soldier shot "Red" Hill, a local law enforcement officer who threatened him unjustly. Ignorant Negroes from the "backwood," who had never before realized that they didn't have to suffer so much injustice, learned it in the army and came back with chips on their shoulders for anything white. So did the war become real to us.

15. Rough Road

THE PASSING MONTHS saw an increase in our anxiety and worry. Friend after friend left for the armed services, until our co-educational college seemed more like Miss Pratt's School for Girls. Junior was deferred until he finished college because he was in his senior year when his call came and was majoring in chemistry. Then he too went away. The house seemed lonely, strange and horribly empty. It made us wonder what it was like on the other side, where members of families were not merely separated but killed, where homes were not just emptied, but destroyed. It was a thought that filled us with horror and even fear, as we realized what could happen here.

I saw many friends and people whom I knew turn to God in this new trial, although heretofore they, like me, had neglected Him. There was increased meaning and fervor at school even in our compulsory devotional exercises. At chapel daily there was a prayer for peace, or for the safety of loved ones in the armed services, or for strength and unity of our country and wisdom for the men who were her leaders. There was less "cutting" of chapel. Now when you heard the many voices lifted in the unison of prayer, or that silence that was even truer prayer, you knew that these people were really talking to God and meaning what they said.

However, at that time religion was still a thing of "feeling" to me. I felt no need of God, so I thought I had none. He was becoming more and more unreal to me, so much so that I felt a scornful contempt for those who, having ignored Him for so long, now turned to Him for consolation because the bottom had dropped out of everything else. It seemed to me a terrible cheat, that we should forget all about God when we were happy; then go whining to Him for help when everything else failed.

Maybe my stepfather was right, I thought; maybe religion was just a drug to dull our senses to realities, especially unpleasant realities. I did not know that, in this sense, God is always "cheated," for we never go to Him in our perfection, justice or worth, but only in His mercy. I did not know that in His mercy He accepts even our meanest offering when it is all we have to give, or that He is always willing to give Himself to us, whenever we will receive Him.

So, filled with pride and a smug self-satisfaction, I continued seeking a perfection wholly worldly and completely separate from the perfection of God. War was just one of the rough roads over which I must walk to obtain it.

16. Waitress

I was sixteen and a college freshman when the appeal for nurses and the Cadet Nurses began to interest the girls in my school. Many of my classmates sent for literature, and everyone was talking about it. At first I was not interested, because I already knew what I wanted to do. I had always wanted to write. I knew I needed something else, though, since writing is such an uncertain profession, at least in the beginning, so for several years I had been wavering between law and medicine. I liked law better, but I didn't like politics, which I considered crooked. But as the months passed, I did grow interested in the C.N.C., having heard so much about it. I talked to my parents and stepfather about it, seeking their advice. Daddy gave his approval and said I could go when I was eighteen (minimum age), and that I should study those courses which would help me most in this meanwhile. That was more than a year off, however, so I continued to go to school.

But opposition came from my stepfather. "Anything but nursing!" he said. "You aren't strong enough. You're too good for that. Why don't you be a doctor? A nurse is nothing, the one who does the dirty work. The doctor gets the money and the credit. With your temper, you'll be out in six months," and so on, and on. "I'm not going to help you throw your life away. You'll get no help from me as far as nursing is concerned. The only thing I'll do is send you your fare to come home."

About this time my father married again, and that strengthened my determination. My stepmother was polite and friendly, but it was the distant, polite friendliness of a stranger. None of us had heard anything of the contemplated marriage until it was all over, so we were not prepared. I welcomed the chance and the excuse to get away from home for awhile rather than make this new adjustment to my way of life so suddenly.

That summer I worked as a waitress in Memphis to earn my fare and initial entrance fee. It was hard work, but not new to me, for I had done similar work, off and on. The customers (most of the regular "good" ones) were hotel or railroad men. They knew me and knew why I worked. They went out of their way to help me, to show me their respect and approval. Often they defended me against some drunken man who wanted to get "fresh":

"Let her alone, can't you see she's just a kid!"

"Don't mind him, Little Bit, that guy is so lowdown he doesn't know when someone's on the level or on the up and up when he sees it."

Sometimes they would tell me: "You know, I wasn't always like this. I got to drinking and running around with the wrong crowd, and here I am."

Or maybe: "You know, kid, a man will do a lot of things for money. And it gets easy after a while to sell almost anything. Then, finally, one day you wake up and see you're hardly a man any more. People who are good, who are on the up and up, don't speak to you, don't want you any more. You're down and out. You get to drinking to forget. And you keep going lower and lower like there ain't no bottom." And he'd take another drink. Or maybe cry.

At the end of the summer I went back to school and studied until February. Then I left Memphis to go to Harlem Hospital in New York City as a Cadet Student Nurse.

17. The Vocation of Nursing

I WAS DISAPPOINTED in New York. It was too big, cold and unfriendly. I didn't like the many dirty streets of Harlem, nor its stark naked apartments, all ugly imitations of one another. I felt sorry for the children who had to grow up there with never a yard to play in nor a tree to climb, nor meadow or woodland to explore, but only the formal parks with their "Keep Off" and "Forbidden" signs.

The hospital itself was not so bad. It was homelike in the nurses' home. The other students were very friendly. Many of them were also from out of town.

I found that my stepfather had been right in some things, but he was wrong in many more. There were things I didn't like, things which I found hard. There was the very heavy class schedule, concentrated to meet the need for nurses during the war, the bite of homesickness and the ordinary difficulties of adjustment to living conditions in a group.

But hardest of all was to learn to obey authority—often an unquestioning, apparently senseless obedience. I have never found it easy to give up my will, and there, all at once, someone else was deciding when I would rise, study, work, play, sleep and eat; and even off duty, it was decided for me where I would go, and often with whom, what clothes I would wear and what time I would return. On duty the obedience was even stricter, since intelligent obedience might mean the difference between life and death for a patient.

Many times, weary, angry, disgusted or disillusioned, I was ready to give it up and go home. Two things stopped me: one was that old pride: I could not bear to hear "I told you so"; nor could I bear to admit failure even to myself. The other reason was a better one. I liked nursing. I liked the responsibility and the human contacts. I liked the feeling of being a part of the struggle for life which was like communion with the Infinite.

The first time I saw a baby being born, I almost cried, because I thought surely he must be dead after all that struggle. Then suddenly he cried, and I felt a wild exultation that made even my unbelieving heart lift in praise.

The first time I saw a patient die, I was filled with awe. I could not believe in death. It seemed impossible that one moment an old woman should be alive and the next moment dead. Even as I cared for her body, I half expected her to start breathing again. I looked at her and wondered about eternity and mused on the possibility of Heaven and Hell. For the first time I saw how pitifully inadequate and helpless we creatures are before the great realities of life and death: not all the brilliant doctors, new "miracle" drugs and scientific discoveries could give this one woman life again. It was a jolting thought.

Birth and death, they were the outstanding events, the jolting ones, but the influence of the monotonous everyday struggle against death and sickness was no less great. And my own part in this struggle gave me a sense like that of junior partnership with the Source of all life, Whom I was still reluctant to call God.

But despite all my uncertainty, anger, weariness and disgust, one thing soon became clear to me: I wanted to be a nurse whatever the cost. Nursing was my vocation.

18. The Lonely Year

THE FIRST YEAR in nursing school was a lonely year. Of course, there were some days that were full and complete—days when there were entertainments or outings sponsored by the school or one of the classes, friendly discussions "after hours" when the lights should have been out and the students in bed, tricks played on one another—like the time I put the laboratory skeleton in one of the students' beds.

Some days we had impromptu parties. A group of us would go up to the penthouse, where there was a kitchen, and cook something—such as cake, or banana pudding, or chili con carne—then bring it down to the rest of the class. As we ate, we talked. Sometimes we guessed at each other's futures. We printed the guesses, together with other funny or interesting things that happened to our class, in my "Naughty-graph" book. The predictions for my own future ranged from "an inmate in Bellevue" and "a neurotic old maid" to "assistant to our educational head" and "the wife of Mr. C." (Mr. C. was one of my former classmates at Rust. I had almost married him several times, but always at the last moment I had been unable to reconcile my conscience with the act, because he was divorced and my ideas about divorce and remarriage had not changed. As far as I was concerned, that unknown girl whom I had never seen and had no desire to see was still his wife, and all the things I was still saying to myself could not change that a bit. I was not fooling myself. That was why this prediction seemed to me as dubious as the preceding one.)

Other days we made fun of ourselves or each other, the faculty or the strict rules of the school. We lived on the sixth floor, and during one time of great upheaval between the students and faculty (which finally ended in many changes in the school and faculty, including the appointment of a new superintendent of nurses) we made a "Memorial Sixth Floor Address":

"Twelve months and seven days ago, our class brought forth to this school a new attitude conceived in bravado and dedicated to the proposition that all student nurses were created efficient.

"We are now engaged in taking final examinations, testing whether those students, or any students so resolved and so involved, can long endure.

"We are met in a great hallway of that school . . ." and so on and on, in parody of the Gettysburg Address. We thought it was very funny; certainly most of it was a true description of our class.

Sometimes one of the girls would take her cake and go back to her room to study, or wash out those garments she didn't send to the hospital laundry. If it were Scott who left, she would sing at the top of her voice, "Oh Baby, won't you please come home?" The rest of us would laugh and tease her about it, and most often it would start a conversation about men:

"Did you see that new patient on 2C? Hubba, hubba!"

"Did I see him? Boy, if he wasn't a patient!"

"Boy, whoever made up these movies about nurses and patients must never have seen a hospital!"

"Not one with Jessie Ruff anyway: 'Now, ladies, remember that professional ethics is from here on to be your guide of conduct. You are to hold yourself up. You are to give every patient the most complete nursing care, but your relationship is to remain at all times impersonal. A sick man is likely to say a lot of things he doesn't mean in his gratitude to the one who has cared for him. Pay this no attention. Do not let me hear of any of you making dates with your patients, is that clear?' 'Yes, Mrs. Ruff.' "

We all laughed. It was certainly a good imitation of our educational head, even the tone of voice.

"But did you see that blond on my ward? Gosh, if I were white I don't know if I'd try to remember he was just a patient or not! Those eyes!"

"Speaking of white, I heard we almost had a white student here recently. Someone advised her against it."

"Yeah, I heard that. Funny we have white doctors and white kitchen help and attendants, lab technicians and things, but only colored nurses and students."

"Wait till you get to Seaview and Bellevue on your affiliations, you'll have all the white students you want and more too."

"Oh, I'm not anxious. Talking about white doctors, what do you think about that new intern?"

"Hubba, hubba!"

"He could make me forget I'm colored."

"Yeah? I know who I'm going to tell that!"

"You can't tell him anything about me. He knows who I want. We are getting married when he comes home on his furlough."

"I'm glad they let student nurses marry here now, yet I don't think I'd want to get married before I finished training. Too many things can happen."

"Things like what?"

"Oh, you know. Babies and things."

"Babies! Didn't you ever hear of a thing called Birth Control? Where were you when the rest of us were taking Gyn?"*

"Ah, she's a Catholic. They don't believe in Birth Control."

"Well, no one is going to tell me how many babies to have unless they are going to support some of them, you can bet your life on that!"

"Me neither."

"Ah, let her alone; when she starts having them every year, she'll forget all that stuff. I know a lot of Catholics who have."

"Let the girl's religion alone."

"How about a game of cards, huh?"

"No, I'm going out with Bill tonight, and I have to dress."

"And I have *got* to study. Did you see my last marks? Boy!"

Some of the days were like that. But mostly it was a lonely year.

No place, I think, is as lonely as a big city to a stranger. So many people, so many sights to see, so many things to do—but none of the people care about you, and it's not much fun going the places or doing the things alone, after a while. You grow weary of living vicariously the superficial lives of the movie heroes and heroines. You go to a museum, and a sculpture or painting fills you with joy and something like awe, and you want to share that thing you feel, but there's no one there to share it. You go to a concert, and as long as the music lasts, you are

* Gynecology.

in another world peopled by the wonderful, friendly people and places of your imagination, but when the last echo dies away, you are more alone than ever. And so it goes for all the amusements the city has to offer.

If you are a man, I guess you especially miss a woman's companionship; if you are a woman, it is just the reverse. Of course, this loneliness is intensified if you've always been used to many friends, admiration and acclamation.

If you are a Negro, as well as a stranger, it's worse, especially if you are a Southern Negro, accustomed to the warm friendliness of people. You know that first-class restaurants, hotels, theaters, etc., have always Jim-Crowed you, or carried unwritten signs, "White Only." You know that even in New York, many places have the same unwritten sign, and you don't know which places they are. You know some but not all.

You shrink from the pain and embarrassment of going where you aren't wanted, where managers simply "don't see" dark patrons, or where tickets are always "out," seats always "sold." You're hungry, but you pass the fine, big, clean-looking restaurants with tablecloths and flowers because you don't see any other colored people there and you don't know—maybe that's one of the places forbidden to you.

So you go to one of the side streets to a cheap-looking one, or maybe stop for a hot dog and drink at Nedick's. Maybe there's a clean-looking colored soldier, sailor or marine there who seems just as lonely and lost as you. Sometimes you return his smile; sometimes you just pretend not to see him. If you smile back, he might come and talk to you.

Most of the girls in my class were strangers, as I was. A few girls met the brothers of other students, home on

(63)

furlough. A few made friends among the young internes. Some stayed alone. Others made friends with the hospital help, secretly, for this was strictly against the rules. Some met young men at the U.S.O., where we could go in our cadet uniforms, or at an indoor swimming pool, where we went almost every day.

In such ways as these we found desired companionship. Many times, after only a few weeks, however, we discovered that the "desired companionship" was not so desirable after all, since too often a man wanted more than he had a right to expect from a mere companion.

With one or possibly two exceptions, I found the men I met like this—superficial, sensual, or both. Maybe it was the war which had created or strengthened in them the desire for conversation without thought, and pleasure without responsibility. They wearied me with their too obvious flattery and overworked platitudes.

Yet I did not shun their company for that reason, but preferred boredom to loneliness, and tried to imagine that they were what I wanted, swallowing my distaste like bad coffee.

19. Beginnings of a Nurse

WHEN WE FIRST entered nursing school, most of our time was spent in study. There was Anatomy, Chemistry, Diet Therapy, Materia Medica, Nursing Arts, Ethics, History of Nursing, Hygiene, Swimming, Microbiology, Sociology and Psychology. As we finished one course, another was added. Actually, for the first six months we saw the wards but rarely and had little to do on them except make beds for patients who were getting better and no longer needed special attention. As the months passed, however, we were given more and more responsibility. We began to give our own patients complete morning and evening care, and to chart. We were given the patients who were very ill if they did not require any treatment beyond those we had so far been taught. We began to assist the doctor in giving treatments and to accompany him on his rounds whenever we could. We learned to pour medications and to calculate dosages ordered from dosages on hand. We learned to call the priest for the dying and to care for the bodies of the dead. We learned how to talk to the relatives or friends of the patients, to insure their cooperation with what we were trying to do. We learned also to teach the patient some of the things he needed to know for his future good health or his present welfare, to help him get well. We learned to take the responsibility of a ward alone in the evenings with only an attendant to help us, and a kitchen girl. That was a strange and awful feeling that came from the knowledge that forty patients were depending on you, on your intelligent actions and decisions. Of course, there was always the supervisor, who could be called if you found yourself in a situation you couldn't handle, and usually there was a graduate nurse on the floor on another ward who would help you if you really needed it, but the decision was up to you. You had to decide to call the doctor, another more experienced nurse or student, or the supervisor. The patients looked to you for what they needed. You were only a student, but to them you were "nurse."

"Nurse, I've got an awful pain in my stomach around that dressing, I wonder if I could get it changed or have a clean combine?"

"Nurse, give me something for my pain, please!"

"Nurse, I'm hungry, but I can't eat this stuff!"

"Nurse, if my husband comes up to talk to the doctor, let him come in for a few moments, hear? Please, I know it's against the rules—but couldn't you?"

"Nurse, I can't sleep."

You knew that they looked up to you; that they depended on you; that they trusted you; and it was a new feeling, a little frightening. But it was a good feeling.

In February, one year after we had entered the nursing school, my classmates and I, standing in semi-darkness, took the Florence Nightingale pledge, and received the symbolic caps of our school.

To most nurses, "capping night" is the most important night of their training period—perhaps of their life as a nurse—much more important than graduation, because it is the true beginning. People graduate from all kinds of schools into many different professions, but capping is exclusively and essentially a part of the nursing profession: of purity, knowledge and service.

The capping ceremony is one of mystery and symbolism. Candles light the room and senior students bearing lighted tapers escort junior students bearing unlit candles to the place where they are to be capped. As the student receives her cap, her candle is lighted from that of the senior student, to signify the passing down of the traditions of nursing. Our lives must show forth as a flaming light, and darkness or stain must not touch them. We must be willing to bear this light down into the dusty shadows of death and pain, and take warmth and brightness there. From one generation of nurses to the next, the flame of charity and service must never be extinguished, but handed down forever.

To me nursing could never again be, if it ever had been, just another job, a way of making money, a substitute for something else, a means to an end. It was something very special, in a class by itself. As we said the pledge, the words branded themselves upon our minds:

"I solemnly pledge myself before God . . . to pass my life in purity . . ." Purity! Poor, neglected, laughed-at virtue these days! I wondered that my lips could even shape themselves to form the word, so unworthy were they to say it. We were promising integrity, purity of body, mind and intention in lives unspoiled and unstained by sensual or selfish motives.

". . . I will not take nor knowingly administer any harmful drug . . ." We handled so many harmful drugs— how easily we began to take them for granted, how often we are tempted to handle them carelessly, thoughtlessly.

(67)

As I said the words, I never dreamed that the time would come when only the grace of God and the faith of a friend would enable me to keep those words.

". . . I will abstain from all that is harmful and deleterious . . . and will hold in confidence all private matters and family affairs coming to my knowledge in the practice of my profession." These words gladdened me, and I said them with feeling. I hoped that at least everyone in my class would keep that part of the pledge. Gossip is hateful and ugly from any person, but gossip from a nurse is unpardonable, especially when it concerns her patient. She is to give comfort and peace, not take it away. Hers is the hand to heal, not to wound.

". . . with loyalty will I endeavor to aid the physician in his work . . .," we continued, and soon were silent again. It was over. The pledge was given. The dedication was made.

The ceremony was over, but our work was just beginning. Yet I doubt if any of us realized then what great possibilities lie in this work. We were being given a share in Our Lord's great work of healing the sick, of comforting those who mourn, and bringing order to disorder. Into our keeping would be given not only bodies and minds, but sometimes souls.

Our hands would receive the newborn infant. Our hands would care for the aged body. Our hands would comfort the dying and close the eyes of the dead. Sometimes our hands would administer the sacrament of Baptism to the dying, and give life to the spiritually dead. Always our voice would summon the priest, and sometimes our hands became like the hands of the priest, bearing life.

I looked at my hands. They seemed terribly small, awkward and clumsy, to do so much. Yet I had promised. I had dedicated myself to this task. I had promised "before God" and in the presence of witnesses. I thought of the parable of the talents. Nurses are given many talents. Some day Our Lord will ask us to account for them. I prayed for grace to spend them well in the service and love of God and my fellows, though I didn't call it grace then, nor my unvoiced yearning, prayer.

20. Is There a God?

THERE IS NO PLACE like a hospital for growth if you want to grow, and a big hospital like ours was a world in itself. Every human problem and every class and personality were represented.

There were infants and grandfathers. There were hardened criminals with police guards. There were ordinary people of all races, creeds and social backgrounds; possibly there was even a saint or two; surely there were some very holy and good people.

Every day marked the ending of life and every day marked the beginning of life. There were hope and faith that made you want to go down on your knees; there were bitterness and despair that stifled even pity, and made you want to turn your eyes away and not see. There were love and hate. There were cowardice and courage. There was most clearly seen the dignity of man and his likeness to His Creator; and then there were men stripped naked of all dignity and become like beasts that have no souls. Is it possible that in such an atmosphere one should not think of God?

My classmates and I often spoke about Him. We were all Christians of some denomination or other, but we actually knew pitifully little about Him and were vague and indefinite about the little we knew.

Was there really a God and was Christ God? Or was

it possible that all sacred history was a myth, a lie that had survived the tests of time and critical examination? Did the whole world and its inhabitants and all the rigid, unchanging laws of time, space and matter evolve from nothingness? Or did God create them? If there was nothing, how could there be laws rigid, timeless and ordered? If there was something, why did some of these laws often seem senseless and almost spiteful? Why was there destitution, suffering and injustice for the just and faithful? Was faith vain—or was faith our only hope of bringing order to chaos, light to darkness and joy to sorrow?

Sunday morning a group of us might be in one room, reading the funny papers, talking, or simply relaxing lazily.

"Where is Kelly?"

"Gone to church. You might know. Williams too."

"Funny, at home I used to go to church pretty regularly myself."

"Me too, but you get away and there are so many things to do you just don't seem to have time any more. Besides, you get so tired, you just don't feel like doing anything on your day off."

"If there is a God, I guess He must understand about those things."

"Maybe so, maybe not. I'm not saying there is or there isn't, but if Christ is God, I guess He got pretty tired too, sometimes, but He didn't give up. He must not have felt much like dying. I know I wouldn't. And if I were dying to save people like me, I don't know that I would have thought it worth the trouble. I wouldn't have bothered. I don't make fun of anyone who goes to church every Sunday like Kelly; I envy her her faith. I wish I could believe. There is too much, though, that doesn't add up—contradictions, things like that. What do you think, Caldwell?"

"I don't know. I guess I believe in God in a way, but it's not the way the preachers have it. I've heard people like Reverend Powell speak of Christ and Christianity and been impressed and joined the church. But it hasn't lasted; I go on back to my own belief because I see that they haven't really a better one to offer me. God is too convenient. But if He can serve their convenience, He might just as well serve mine. There are few things that I believe are absolutely right or wrong. As a matter of fact, sometimes I wonder if there are any such things. It is the integrity of yourself, your own being, that is important. If you believe something is right or good, it's got to be right and good for you. If you believe that something is wrong, then you can't do it, that's all; not without being a traitor to your own self, not without losing yourself.

"You can do what you want; have what you want; but you've got to understand that everything has its price, and when you take something you've got to pay for it. The bigger it is, the more it's going to cost."

"If that were true, it would mean that God didn't care much about what happened in His world."

"Do you think He cares?" The words were contemptuous.

"You don't really think He loves us, then, or cares what happens or what people do?" another girl asked curiously.

"Look around you," I suggested. "The Negro slave believed and prayed, and the black man has been praying ever since. What has it got him? Did you ever read Countee Cullen? He has the right idea. Look at the world

(72)

now and answer your own question. Do *you* think He cares?"

"Yet if what you say is true, then everything that Christians have been taught for centuries is a mockery; but the Bible says 'God is not mocked.'"

"Then maybe He mocks. At times, it would seem so."

"And you've got nerve enough to call yourself a Christian?"

"If that's not blasphemy, I don't know what is."

"You think I am bad, that that's blasphemy? You should have heard the preacher who taught us Bible at school. Was Jesus God as the Father is God? Was He born of a virgin? Were His miracles really miracles, or are they outstanding coincidences and metaphor, parables? Was He really dead, or could there be some doubt? He seemed to think 'no' to all the questions which I bet you will all say 'yes' to. 'Jesus was a Man, a holy Man, no more. He was born naturally of the relationship between Mary and Joseph, not at all uncommon or improper in those days.' Why Joseph was surprised then, I couldn't say. 'The miracles weren't really miracles, because,' he says, 'God does not go against His own laws, and a miracle is against the law of nature.'"

"I've heard them like that too, but I don't believe it. If Jesus wasn't God, I don't think He was a very holy man to go about saying He was."

"There are so many questions—I wonder if anyone knows the answer to any of them?"

"If there is, I only hope I meet him or her before I die."

"There is Father Divine; he says he knows the answers. In fact he claims he *is* the answer, God personified, Father Divine."

"Oh, Father Divine! How could anyone stoop so low?"

(73)

"He does a lot of good, though; look what he has done for the poor. You used to be able to get a dinner there for fifteen cents that you'd pay a dollar for somewhere else. He's not all bad."

"I wonder what happens to a person like that when he dies?"

"They say, his followers I mean, that he won't die."

"If what they say about Hell is true, I guess he'd better not."

"Daddy Grace is another one like him. Miracles, so they claim, of healing and fortune. Got their own Heaven too, with black angels."

"Guess the rest of the world is Hell."

"Sure seems like it sometimes!"

"But they seem happy. We have a patient on our ward who's one of Father Divine's followers, ignorant and poor, but she doesn't complain. Says she is happy, Father is Divine, and peace, it's wonderful!"

"Some people are easily satisfied. They are like sheep. They will follow anybody with the strength or interest to lead them. How does the Bible put it—'Lambs led to the slaughter'?"

"They are children, though, no matter how old they get to be; with them any kind of God, if He loves man at all, must be merciful. Hell, if it exists, couldn't be for them."

"No, I've heard that it is reserved for the proud."

"Caldwell, that sounds like you! Imagine—reservations!"

"I wouldn't be surprised. Seriously, though, I believe that there is Something, not necessarily Someone, but Something. The world is cockeyed, and a lot of things don't make sense; but they are impossible without that

Something. Something has to keep and create what little order there is. Maybe it is not a person, but it has to be intelligent. Maybe that's the answer. It can think, but It can't feel. Maybe It doesn't understand about pain and sorrow and suffering. Or maybe It understands and knows but doesn't care."

"Or maybe It understands, knows and cares, but can't do anything about it."

"Could be. Call It an Intelligence. Call It Universal Mind or Soul. Call It a Spirit. Or call It God. It doesn't matter. It is there. Maybe our own souls are a part of It."

"Then you do believe in a soul?"

"Believe? Have you ever taken care of the body of a patient who has died and felt that here was just an empty shell under your hand, that something was there once and is now gone? Did you ever feel that it was still nearby, looking over your shoulder, maybe? Did you ever find yourself turning quickly to see it there behind you, feeling foolish afterwards? But at the same time, didn't you feel that this intangible something was just as real as that limp thing under your hand?"

"So you have felt that, too?"

"Who among us has not? The question is what has gone and where did it go and how did it get there in the first place?"

"The question is, did God make it, create it, or was it always in existence in one form or another?"

"The question is, If God did make it, why?"

"Or you could say the question is, If God did make it, was it just to amuse Himself, or did He have some care and thought for it. Having made it, did He love or hate what He had made?"

Such deep questions for such little people! But we did

not feel little. We knew that the questions were deep, and that great minds through the ages from the beginning of time have sought the answer to those questions with never a completely satisfactory answer to all; but as much as anyone needed the answer, we needed it.

As far as God and eternity are concerned, there are no little nor great minds, but just the human need to know the human end, since our lives are necessarily directed toward what we believe our end to be. We live according to what we believe of God, that's why it is so important that what we believe be true. If we believe we are mere animals, we will live as mere animals. If we believe that we are sons of God, we will try to live as sons of God. So we sought the answer.

I did not believe that a logical, orderly world came haphazardly into being from nothing or from blind cosmic forces; nor that thought and reason could have had a birth from other than thought and reason.

Looking upon death again and again, I could not believe that it was the end of all being. The *body* which I saw was not the *person* I had known. Something had been there; now it was gone—not annihilated, but gone away from its dwelling place. Where? I did not know. What? I supposed it was the soul.

Alone in my own room, or in my quiet moments on duty or outside, I thought over some of the things which had been said in discussions with classmates, or which I had been reading. I wondered about the real meaning and purpose of life as well as its source. It may sound strange, but I never prayed for faith or enlightenment. I don't know if I knew that one could pray for those things. I suspect I was just so filled with a proud self-sufficiency and spirit of independence that I liked to find or make my own way. I didn't want to be shown or helped by anyone, not even by God.

Fortunately, God does not give His help, even the grace of faith, only to those who are worthy. For none are worthy, but He gives His help, freely, to all who seek him sincerely. Humility is necessary, but a certain amount of grace is necessary too, before even humility is possible. That minimum of grace He gives to all those who seek Him, and it is often to those least worthy that He gives most generously.

I suppose He could find no one less worthy than myself, so He gave me the beginnings of grace, richly and generously.

Soon I was sure of three things: there is a God, Christ is His Son, and my own need of Him was most acute. I did not even know where to start looking for Him. I couldn't find Him; but I hoped He would find me. And He did.

21. Why Does God Permit Suffering?

"OUGHT NOT CHRIST to have suffered these things and so entered into His glory?"

Those were Our Lord's words to His troubled disciples who had been scandalized by His Passion, Cross and Death. It did not fit into their preconceived false notions of what the Christ was to be like. Even after all His teaching, even after having lived with Him for three years, they still did not understand Him—and neither do we after twenty centuries. Instead, suffering is a stumbling-block to us as it was to them. He accepted it as a matter of course, something that is a part of our fallen state. Not admitting a fallen state, we are unable to accept it at all.

It was a stumbling-block to me also. Sometimes I was appalled and terribly depressed by the constant stream of human misery that passed before me in the hospital. With a passion of bitterness, I stormed against whatever muddling, senseless, sadistically spiteful Power was responsible for it.

Why did God permit suffering? Was He powerless to prevent it, or was it that He just didn't care?

Here was a newly married young man, clean, decent, honest, looking forward to a bright future he hoped to have with his wife and the children they both wanted—

accidentally scalded and horribly burned from the waist down. He would never father those children; if he lived, he would be fortunate even to work and walk again. But he didn't even want to live.

There was a young mother who had so wanted the baby which was born hopelessly deformed in body and mind.

Here was a young girl, homeless, poor, deserted by family and friends because the tiny mite she hugged so hungrily to her had no legitimate father.

There was an infant born blind and abandoned in the hospital.

Here was a woman with incurable cancer, in constant pain, who seemed unable either to live or to die.

To what purpose was all this? That there was so much suffering like this and worse, what did it mean? Couldn't God see it? Couldn't He prevent it? Then why didn't He? He must not care.

There were times when I sensed something of the meaning of suffering, and knew that it is not always as senseless and purposeless as it seems at first glance, nor always an evil.

Having accepted the fact that Christ is God, I had no alternative but to see in suffering at least some possibility of good, since He also suffered. The cross was real and His suffering was real. It's funny how easily most of us forget this. We are not saddened by the fact that Christ is crucified, so much as by the fact that He is crucified in us and those we love.

A Christian loves Christ and tries to live his life as Christ lived His on earth. But I came to realize that this isn't all. All the Christians who have lived since He died to redeem men from sin continue His life on earth. He lives in them. As St. Paul says, "With Christ I am nailed to the cross. It is now no longer I that live, but Christ that lives in me." We, Christians, together make up His real body now. He is the Head. And if we are His Body, He suffers again in us. And even we must admit that the suffering of God could not be vain or senseless. His act of redemption is continued, as it were, in the sufferings of Christians, who together are what St. Paul defines as the Mystical Body of Christ.

Of course I didn't know all these things then, or see suffering in this light, but I did see that good often comes from suffering. I had seen it make weak people strong and give courage to cowards. I had seen it reconcile enemies and strengthen the love of friends. I had seen it change hateful, intolerant people and make them gentle and understanding. I had seen it humble the proud and exalt some poor weak creature who bore it well. I had seen it bring out the best and worst in those who suffered and those who stood by, stripping away all pretension and lies and leaving only the bare truth.

I myself had made the statement (and heard others make similar statements) that I wished my beloved younger brother would go to war so he could "grow up." I meant that I wished he would have a little suffering to strengthen him. So I did know, when I would admit it, that suffering can lead to good.

I could also see that much of our suffering is of our own making, though I did not like to admit this. Even those who will not admit the existence of a moral law must admit the fact of a natural law which we all transgress from time to time. And when we break laws, we must pay the penalty. Many of my patients were paying the supreme price for having transgressed, however involuntarily, some law of health.

But most of all, there was the suffering of Christ. I could not shut my eyes to that. He Who should have been free from all suffering had voluntarily suffered and died for our redemption. That was something to think about. Perhaps there could be something redeeming in our suffering, also. Thus did I grope my way toward the light.

I thought that I could see a part of the answer to suffering, that is, why God permits it. He permits it for the same reason He permits sin or any act or part of our lives, because it fits into the master plan of creation which is His secret alone. Our task is not so much to answer the why of suffering, but rather to find out how we can use it for good, and like Our Lord, so enter into our glory.

22. What Is Death?

I IMAGINE that the thought of death fills almost everyone with a sense of awe and strangeness, if nothing else. Even those who must see it nearly every day never get used to it. When you do see it so often, a time does come when you can accept it without losing your outward calm and serenity, but inside it always leaves a queer, empty, helpless feeling.

It always filled me with a sort of wondering incredulity and an awe that was partly fear. It humbled me as nothing else could. In the presence of death I had to acknowledge my own and all human limitations. I had to admit that there are some things that we can neither understand nor control. Death is universal and inevitable, and old as Adam, yet what do we know of it? Scientists who are unwilling to admit the existence of a soul find it difficult even to define. Perhaps it is this strangeness which frightens us.

When I first went into nursing, I hated even the thought of death. It seemed to me something horrible, an evil that might some day be vanquished. I thought it too morbid to discuss except in ghost stories and the like. But in time this attitude changed completely. I found myself freely joining in the conversations and discussions of death that often took place in the students' rooms when we were off duty.

"That girl died on three south."

"Oh, no! You mean the one who took poison?"

"Um humm. That one. It's a damn dirty shame, a young kid like that with everything to live for."

"Did she ever regain consciousness?"

"No, she slept on till the end. I gave her Coramine and she was getting CO_2 and oxygen all the time. It wasn't any use, though."

"No, I guess not. When your time's up, I guess you got to go."

"Yeah, funny too, nobody, none of us can tell either, but our own is running out. Remember that boy on 3C? He was always cursing his family, God, the doctors and nurses, everybody. I don't guess he thought his was up."

"Guess not. Wonder what happens to a fellow like that afterwards—"

"Providing there is an afterwards, you mean."

"Okay, providing there is."

"If there's a Hell, I'll bet lots of people's there."

"Sure. You know what they say. Heaven for climate, Hell for company."

(There was general laughter at this.)

"It's queer—with all we know in science and medicine, with all we can do, we don't know any more about death really than our grandpas, and they no more than the Ubangi. I wonder if we'll ever know how to stop death or create life?"

"Hardly," one girl might answer, the edge of her faith not dulled or blunted like most of ours. "I think God reserves the power over life and death to Himself. He gives us, I think, only power over suffering."

Then we might go into a discussion of suffering. You can't work in a hospital very long without seeing that sometimes death is the only possible relief from suffering. You work for life, you fight and sweat for it, you try to fan every spark you find left, if it's only the will to live. Yet you know that death will be welcome, and you almost pray for it to come soon. You try to make its coming as easy and natural as possible. If the patient is a Catholic, you call the priest. If he is not, you ask him if he wants a minister, and call one if he does.

Seeing these things, you have to realize that death is not always an evil. Yet it still did not seem to me the possible path to a good that was lasting. It took an infant to teach me this.

23. "I Baptize Thee . . ."

I HAD ALWAYS been especially horrified by infant suffering and death. It seemed to me most senseless and useless, most painful. Why should the innocent suffer, or why should life be cut off before it had even begun? Life seemed so sweet to me that I could not bear to think of anyone's being denied a full taste of its sweetness. And if death ended everything, what did we have?

But suppose it didn't? Suppose there really was a Heaven and infants could go there; wouldn't that make even the briefest life worthwhile? It was something to ponder, anyway. I wondered about it, if only about my own part in it.

We were taught from the time we began our pediatrics and obstetrics classes that we must baptize all unbaptized infants of Catholic parentage, if they were in danger of death, even those tiny, half-formed little ones of miscarried pregnancies, no matter how short the duration of the pregnancy. In our hospitals this was a rule that was very strictly enforced, too. The fact that most of the staff were non-Catholic only emphasized the importance with which it was regarded. And this impressed me most.

The first time I was called upon to administer the sacrament I held the little one on one arm and gently poured a little water over his head, as one of the Catholic chaplains, Father Stocker, had explained to us, repeating, as I had been taught:

"I baptize thee, child, in the Name of the Father and of the Son and of the Holy Ghost, Amen." I said it aloud, feeling a little embarrassed, and glad I was alone, with no one to see me.

The baby moved a little, and I wrapped him up and put him on the table. I knew he couldn't live. He was born of a five-months' pregnancy and was little bigger than my hand. As I watched him, it was then, without knowing quite how it happened, that I felt my embarrassment fading, and a fierce pride and joy replacing it, as if he were my own creation of joy. His death was not ugly, but peaceful and easy, almost imperceptible. I couldn't tell exactly when the feeble flame went out. If there was a Heaven, then he was now in it, in the bosom of God. He had never known and would never know sorrow or suffering, but had gone from joy to Joy, from life to Life. And I had been allowed to give him that privilege, that joy, by one simple act, "I baptize . . ."

The thought was good, the feeling one of intense pleasure. It was then that I first began to realize that death need not be terrible at all but could be a bridge to Heaven, to God.

Several times after that I baptized infants who were dying. Never again was I embarrassed or ashamed. Always I rejoiced and felt something like elation, dimmed only by the knowledge that the death would sadden the parents, who had built many fond hopes and dreams on this little one.

Once the infant was what medicine terms a "monstrosity"—that is, an infant whose physical deformities are so great as to render his appearance almost inhuman. This was a little girl. It was not my case, but no one else seemed to pay any attention to her. They were looking

after the mother and staring at the child. Finally, everyone else went away for a while, so I picked her up and
administered the sacrament. I thought as I did so how
sad this child's life would have been if it had been possible for her to live. She would have suffered all the
extremes of mockery and pity and could only have
offered her life as one of suffering. Now she was with
God. She had to be, or there was no meaning to anything.
She could only have been born for this, that she might
be reborn in God.

24. Time to Think

I WAS STILL CAUGHT in my own heedlessness and mad rush to get somewhere without ever thinking where I was going. However, the time came when I had to stop and think. I didn't particularly want to. I had to.

It all started after about nine months of training, when I began to get troublesome sore throats at too-regular intervals. I was losing so much time off duty that finally the doctor said, "Young lady, we're going to remove those tonsils." And within a short time I was out of the nurses's home and into the hospital waiting for a tonsillectomy.

I was alone in bed in a room all day long except for a few minutes at lunch and supper, when some of my classmates came to visit me, and an hour or so at night, when a few other friends I had in the city could visit. There were only three or four days of this, but that can be a long time when you have nothing to do but think. You can see a lot of things about yourself which you have been missing, or maybe deliberately ignoring.

So many things had happened to me in New York that I hardly knew myself any more. I can't say that I had changed greatly; rather, *what I was* had become more obvious. My direction had not changed, but I had come to the place where I could no longer hide from myself the fact that it was the direction that led *away* from God. I was afraid to think where it did lead.

Funny, we say we don't believe in Hell, but we are afraid of it just the same. It is because in our thoughtful moments we perceive that the things which will make Hell such a terrible place are the things which sometimes make the earth a terrible place, and that the paths which lead away from God also lead away from humanity and toward the bestial. Perhaps it is because we see that although sin is primarily an offense against God, there is no sin which does not mark the human personality as well, the sinner himself most of all, and that Hell is full of souls so marked to the point of hideous deformity.

And it was just such marks upon my own body and soul that caught and held my attention, even against my will.

Looking into my own soul, I found still there a desire for God, but one which had been stifled by pride and self-interest and choked by worldly growths. The ugly weeds of sin had so hidden it that I only perceived it by a deep hunger and need for I knew not what, something which I could not define but which I wanted to possess.

I saw new sins of carelessness and indifference added to all my old ones. I saw in myself a person who always wanted things her own way, regardless of the hurt to others, unless their hurt hurt her.

Here was a person who had set for herself as a code of ethics the premise that "Anything I believe is right is right for me." "Right" grew to include more and more, until finally it included nearly anything she wished to do. It had not always been so; once there had been definite laws of truth and integrity, but how easily the laws we make for ourselves degenerate, noble though we may be, when we exclude God from them!

I wasn't even completely truthful any more, something upon which I had always prided myself before, nor kind nor patient with those weaker than myself. On the contrary, I found myself taking a sort of perverse pleasure in hurting some people and exercising my supposed "power" over them. I thought it amusing to trifle with other people's affections while I remained unaffected. Though the year was not over yet, I had already promised myself in marriage to three different men and never meant it once. There were other things too—all in all, not a very pretty picture.

Yet I had always wanted such great things, had set before myself such a real perfection and such high goals, and at first such noble lines of thought and conduct! What had happened to all of that? Suddenly I was faced with the fact of my own limitations and the realization that even those of us who think ourselves most strong and perfect can do nothing good without the help of some Power outside and greater than ourselves; to be specific, without the help of God, known or unknown. It was a humiliating admission to have forced from me, and difficult to make. But humility is the beginning of faith. Perhaps that's why God had given me time to think.

25. New Beginnings

WHILE I WAS STILL a patient in the hospital, one day Father Meenan, another of the Catholic chaplains, stopped at the door of my room as he was making his rounds, to speak to me.

We talked awhile, and finally I found myself telling him something of how mixed up and troubled I was. Perhaps he sensed, or perhaps I told him, something of my growing thirst for faith, for God. He is young, but has a gift for seeing and understanding many things before you have put them into words—which is a good thing for those of us who have trouble saying aloud many of those things which haunt or trouble us.

He agreed that what I was seeking was God and that I needed faith. Before he left, he asked me if I would like to be a Catholic and I said yes. It was as simple as that.

As soon as I was well again, I started going to him for instructions in the faith and for advice in other things as well. One of my classmates, Mac, and sometimes another, Scott or Kelly, went with me, but they only wanted to learn. They did not seek Baptism.

Father Meenan was a good teacher. He reminded me a lot of my father in the way he taught me. He had a great love for poetry and good literature and frequently recommended some to me. He especially liked *The Hound of Heaven.* At the same time, faith and the clear idea of sanctity as the main purpose of life seemed to shine from him, until it became easier for me also to know that reality of God and the certainty of the Catholic faith. Grace worked through him to pour itself into me.

I don't remember finding anything about the faith difficult to accept in theory, though I found some things hard to put into practice, to realize and apply in my own life. I found it easy, for instance, to accept the authority of the Church and of the Holy Father as its head. But I found it hard to feel or give real devotion to the Blessed Mother or the Saints. I believed they truly lived, but I kept thinking of them as "White." I know it sounds impossible that our prejudices could extend even to the supernatural realm, but they can. Prejudice can spread until it is a part of the very air we breathe into our lungs.

While Father Meenan was white, I didn't consider him in the same light. He was set apart, a priest. He was different. He had overcome being white, I was generous enough to admit. I can't imagine why I couldn't extend this narrow "generosity" to the saints, the chosen of God —but then, when was prejudice reasonable?

I thought they wouldn't understand me anyway, these white saints. What does the heart of a white man know of the heart of a black one, or the heart of a saint know of the heart of a sinner? The white, the chosen people of the world, what did they know of or care for my temporal needs? The saints, the chosen of God, what did they know of or care for one who had consistently defied and offended the God they loved? How could there be communion between us or a common meeting place?

It was not until later that I learned that God's love is

our communion, and in Him we meet. When I said the Rosary for Our Lady, or prayers to the saints, it was an act of faith only; the love came later.

So every Wednesday found me going over to St. Mark's for instructions.

"How are Miss Caldwell and Miss McPherson today?"

"Fine, Father."

"That's elegant. Come inside. I found those books for you. Have you been able to get any of the others?"

"Not yet, Father."

"I hope you can, especially Cardinal Newman and Father Leen. I think you will get a lot out of both of them."

"I'm going to try to get them. Father, have you seen that new patient on three south?"

"You mean that young girl?"

"Yes. They say she tried to commit suicide. If she did and if she dies, do you think there can ever be any forgiveness for her?"

"That is the sin of despair, and to die unrepentant is to put yourself beyond forgiveness, to damn yourself. Of course, no one can say in a particular case that someone did not die repentant. It may be that between the act and its accomplishment the person did repent. We can always hope that this was the case and pray for that soul, offering our own sacrifices and sufferings for it. But if there were no repentance . . ." He spread his hands and lifted his shoulders in an expressive gesture, habitual with him. I understood.

"But Father, sometimes it would be easy, I think too easy, to despair; God can seem awfully far away."

"That is a temptation, yes, but we are always given sufficient grace to resist temptation."

(93)

"But suppose you were not?"

"Our Lord says you are."

"But don't you think that there are some people whose heredity or environment has been so terrible that they really can't be any better than they are?"

"Are you talking about normal people, I mean mentally?"

"Yes."

"No. Christ was born and died to make it possible for us to be like Him; He didn't die for nothing."

"But wouldn't that apply only to those who are to be saints? I mean, only a saint would be like God."

Father Meenan smiled. "Only saints go to Heaven," he acknowledged; "but," he added, "only saints are in purgatory, too."

"But that means—!"

"Yes, that means we are *all* called to be saints. Me and you too. Nobody's left out but of his own free will. Now how about your lesson—I think we were going to talk about the commandments of the Church today, weren't we?"

All called to be saints! That was something! You had to think about that. It opened up a whole new world that you had never dreamed of before, and more wonderful than those worlds you had been dreaming of when you dreamed, a world you had never known existed.

I thought of his words then and many times again during those months he instructed me in the Faith. He said them again, too, at different times, in different ways. But always it meant the same. We are all called to be saints!

26. "Do You Renounce Satan?"

AT LAST the day came for which I had waited so long, the day I was to be baptized. Never did days pass so slowly as in the last of those six months of instructions. I desired to receive the sacraments with an intensity greater than mere physical desire. But I was learning patience, too.

When the day came at last, I joined the group which formed the regular catechism class for adults, under Father Kirby. For my sponsor I chose Hyler Spady, one of my nursing supervisors, greatly admired by Father Meenan for her charity. She was one of our favorite nurses too, because of her understanding of young people. Thus fortified, but with dry lips and cowardly knees, I answered the questions preliminary to the reception of the sacrament.

"What do you ask of the Church of God?"

"Faith."

"What does Faith offer you?"

"Life everlasting." I said it, but I don't believe I really thought much about life everlasting in those days. I thought I would be content if it would only enable me to bear well the burdens of this life and make me pleasing to God.

"Do you renounce Satan?"

"I do renounce him."

"And all his pomps?"

"I do renounce them."

I had only the vaguest notion what "all his pomps" might include, but I was sure of this much: I was ending one life, and I wanted to be born clean into a new one. If that meant renouncing some things, possibly even some people as well, which heretofore had meant much, then I meant to do it. Of course, I didn't know how hard that could be; still I felt sure I would receive grace to do it as I repeated those things to myself fiercely:

"I do renounce him, I do renounce them."

"Do you believe in God, the Father . . .?"

"I do believe." Here, at least, was something I could be absolutely certain of.

"Do you believe in Jesus Christ, His only son . . .?"

"I do believe." And this:

"Do you also believe in the Holy Ghost, the Holy Catholic Church, the communion of saints, the remission of sins, the resurrection of the body and life everlasting?"

Surely that was a lot to ask a person to believe. Yet was it, if it was true? Anyway, did I believe it? Could I honestly say I did?

"I do believe."

"Go out of her, unclean spirit, and make room for the Holy Ghost, the Paraclete."

Father Meenan had explained the ritual of Baptism to me, so I could recognize and understand the acts and prayers, and referred me to books which carried further explanations. Now the idea of unclean spirits departing from me was disconcerting. "My name is Legion"—I wondered if there were a whole legion of them departing. Considering my many faults, I thought this quite possible, though such an admission was quite humbling to my pride.

"Will you be baptized?"

Here was something tangible at last, that I could see with outward eyes as well as the inward eyes of faith. *Would I? Of course! What do you think I'm here for, that I've been getting ready for all these months?* And, aloud: "I will."

"I baptize thee . . ."

Here were words I had said, now being said for me; a sacrament I had administered, now being administered to me. I wondered if the babies I had baptized had had something to do with it.

"Receive this white garment . . ."

"Receive this burning light and keep thy Baptism so as to be without blame . . ."

That was like nursing; it reminded me of the candle-lit room on capping night, when another pledge was given. Only this meant so much more. There I had dedicated myself to the service of man, here to the service of God.

"Go in peace, and the Lord be with you."

It was finished. I was a Catholic. Now with my friends I could celebrate my birthday into a new life.

27. Marriage Is a Sacrament

Could it be that we have so lost our vision of the Infinite that we can no longer see marriage as the sacrament which it is, but only as a legitimate or socially acceptable means of satisfying carnal desires, or as "a free partnership between equals, comparable to a business partnership, and which can be dissolved by either partner at will"?

"Is he intelligent, resourceful, ambitious? Is he regularly employed? In a job with some chance for advancement? Is he emotionally and physically mature? Has he a sense of humor? Is he a good sport? Is he concerned principally with the other's happiness? Is the love 'real'?"

Those are the questions which we ask ourselves, and doubtless they are important questions. But we have omitted the most important questions of all, if we are speaking of Christian marriage, of the sacrament. We have failed to ask, "Is he a Christian? Does he have the faith? Is he resolved to make God the center of his being and actions and the guiding force of our marriage?"

Just for the sake of curiosity, I asked the girls in my ward the question, and only *one* made Christian character one of her qualifications for marriage. And I doubt that she did (or would) make that the first, or at least one of the first points to consider.

When faith is considered a purely personal and private

matter, it has limited influence on people. Therefore the presence or absence of Divine love is often outweighed by the presence or absence of human love in our decisions. Yet this ought not to be so, since marriage is a sacrament; that is, by definition, "a holy thing made by Christ to give grace."

I have mentioned the levity with which I treated the thought of marriage, and how lightly I promised myself with no slightest intention of keeping my word. Still, marriage itself had always been sacred to me, if only because I was convinced of its heavenly origin and indissoluble character.

How these conflicting attitudes could exist in the same person is a paradox which I cannot explain. Perhaps I believed that marriage was sacred and love was not, losing sight of the fact that God is the Author of both. That would explain why I could blithely trifle with human affections and emotions with never a qualm of conscience, how I could consider such trifling a dangerously exciting game where I could make all the laws.

When I told George Day I would marry him, I was only fooling at first. There were many things which I didn't know about him—such as his family and social background (that is, his past personal relationships with other people, friends, co-workers, etc.), but I thought this unimportant.

There were a lot of things I did know which did matter too, but I tried to close my eyes to them—things like differences in ideals and attitudes toward right and wrong. To him God was real—an abstraction is real—and so were His laws. He argued, however, that our natural human weaknesses excused us from observing them when they became inconvenient. To me, God was real and His

laws real, not abstractions, convenient or not. But somehow, as my liking for him grew, I imagined I could reconcile our opposite poles of thought and belief. For my
attachment did grow. In looks and personality, ambition
and ability, things we set such high value on, he was desirable, "a catch," so one day I told him in all seriousness
that if he went to Father Meenan to talk to him and
signed the agreement non-Catholics must sign when
marrying Catholics with the approval of the Church
(that the marriage ceremony will be Catholic, the Catholic party will have full liberty to practice his or her own
religion, and the children will be baptized Catholic), I
would marry him.

He made excuses and put it off at first, but finally
agreed to go. So I gave my promise, though with mis-
givings. More than once I told him my doubts, and more
than once he resolved them—or at least stilled them for
a time. So faith and reason bowed for a time to "love,"
to passion.

28. Trouble and Sadness

To TELL OF the things that happened in the next few months between George and me might make this book more interesting, especially to the curious. But it would not make it a better book. It would not further the purpose for which it was written. It could only serve to hurt those who have already been hurt enough by me and who do not deserve this much more from my hands.

It is enough, I think, to say that in our life together we failed miserably to obtain anything good or lasting, for the very simple reason that we looked for the wrong things, and that in the wrong way. I began by compromising my faith, the thing that should have been, and had been until so recently, most precious to me. He began by lying where truth is essential. It was like the house of sand Our Lord describes. We built on nothing, on "love" —as the movies and popular novels define it—that "grande passion" which is justified in itself and so justifies its own actions, *ipso facto*; "And the rain fell, and the winds blew, and they beat upon that house, and it fell, and great was the fall thereof."

Life in the hospital went on just the same. People were admitted and people were discharged; a man was born and another died. There was care to be given, words of comfort to be said, and your deepest problems were your own, closed up inside or revealed in part to a trusted friend whose love was made dumb by an inexperience that wanted to comfort but was mute because it did not know what to say.

Once upon a time when Christians were in distress or troubled with any need, they advised each other to pray that either the troubles be dispelled or they be given the help to bear them for as long as God willed. But now when Christians are troubled, often, like pagans, they advise each other, knowingly: "Get more outside interests; don't think about it; bury yourself in work." So God and prayer are once again pushed to the fringes of our existence while the world seems to triumph in our affections.

It was just such advice as this that most of my friends, except my confessor, gave me when they knew something of the trouble and sadness that had come into my life and seized upon my soul like a lion, until I could cry, like David, "My soul is troubled exceedingly, but Thou, O Lord, how long? . . . Night after night I moisten my bed with weeping; I water my couch with my tears . . ."

I was nearing the end of my second year in nursing school and looking forward with glad anticipation to the reception of the black band which would make me a senior student, when I discovered in myself symptoms that made me certain I was going to be a mother. I began making tentative plans for the arrival of the baby.

Hardly had the doctor assured us that the little one's advent was certain, when his father was arrested by the naval authorities for desertion. I had wondered about the long, frequent shore leaves but accepted his explanation of them without question. Then, after the arrest, deception after deception came to light, until it seemed that all our life together was based on nothing but lies, to each other as well as to outsiders. In a short time I was a very wounded and disillusioned young person.

In my hurt and bitterness, I gave myself up completely to a burning anger and desire for revenge. At first I refused to speak to him at all. When I did agree to see him (at the intercession of his family), it was only to tell him that I didn't want to see him again, that from that day forward I intended to tell everyone that I was a widow and tell my child that his father was dead. I would not say or listen to anything else, but went back to the hospital.

There I was faced with a new problem: how was I going to provide for myself and the baby? I was too proud to go to my mother or father, where I would have to endure the curious stares of neighbors, and what would hurt worse, the pitying looks of friends. It did not seem that I could bear pity from anyone—those I loved, least of all. Pride is indeed a poison, and I was thoroughly intoxicated with it. Later I would be willing to let my mother help me by caring for the baby while I finished school, but first I must stand on my own feet.

29. Work Is a Blessing

FATHERS MEENAN AND KIRBY together helped me to obtain a job as cook and housekeeper in the home of an Irish family in Larchmont, New York. They were a middle-aged couple with one son in New York, studying to be a doctor, and a daughter in a convent. The man's aged mother lived with them, and I also had to look after her a little.

They were all very kind to me. Mrs. McCormick helped me with the difficult part of my work and with caring for her mother-in-law. She gave me things, too—books, including a daily missal which had belonged to her daughter, a pair of ice skates, and some other things.

The work was new but not difficult for me, because they understood my lack of experience and were patient with my shortcomings. I liked to work, felt I had to, and pushed myself mercilessly to find in work forgetfulness, till concern over my baby's welfare or my own stopped me.

When I was not busy I read, or played the piano. They had a good library and a fine old piano, both of which I was free to use in my leisure. There, through the many books in the library, I became acquainted with real saints like John Bosco and Theresa of Lisieux who had fallen in love with God, living, suffering, dying in and for him, yet losing none of their humanity; being tempted as we are tempted, loving as we love—but in a different direction—each communicating in a unique way some perfection of God. That was a part of what I learned.

I learned something else too: I learned that work is a blessing—that it can almost work miracles of healing in wounded souls, that it can bring a measure of peace. Yet day ends and night comes, and finally we must rest. We can work until limbs and muscles ache and cry out in protest, and we think, now we ought to sleep if only from sheer exhaustion. But we don't. We have to face ourselves then, and our problems, in all their terror and ugliness. That's when we need God. That is when we need Him and our faith most of all.

Sometimes, lying there like that, I would think of what I had learned of drugs from my father and in nursing. I thought how easy it is to make and take some of the deadliest. I didn't need a drugstore or a prescription, just my own knowledge of methods of preparation. Daddy had taught us a lot he didn't teach his other students in most cases, because the knowledge can be dangerous for the weak.

I'd think of those things, then remember a candle-lit room and a group of joyous, eager students, pledging in all sincerity there in the dimness with the candlelight on their faces: "*I solemnly pledge myself before God . . . I will not take nor knowingly administer any harmful drug . . .*"

I'd remember my friends too, especially Father Meenan. He believed in me. He had helped me. Through the mercy of God, he had fathered me into the faith, guided and directed me and shown me the clear vision of the Good and Beautiful, seen through his own eyes and communicated to me. And this I wanted to do was against the Good and Beautiful, against both faith and hope.

Then I would find myself praying with real fervor "God help me. My little saints, pray for me. Ask God to do what He wills with me, but ask Him also to give me strength to bear it."

"My little saints" were all the babies I had baptized. They must have answered, because I was kept from despair. God did give me the strength I needed to work, and somehow I was comforted and reassured. Thus does He come to those who seek Him in humility, even in their extremity when they have all but renounced Him.

I say "all but renounced Him" because in me, faith was being born again. It was a slow process; it didn't happen in a night, so that one day I could say "This day have I known Thee." It was like a plant that has been bleached, bruised and broken, hidden away from the sun under a rock, that springs up fresh and strong and green after a time in the sun, when the rock is taken away.

I went to Mass and received the Sacraments at first because it still seemed to me an obligation, then because there I found consolation, and finally because I came to love it. I went to Father Meenan at first because he was my friend and I could talk to him and he would understand, but finally because he was my father in Christ, and by God's grace had brought me to a truer love of God until, loving Him, I wanted His love and wanted to do the things which would please Him more than I wanted to please myself or be comforted or be consoled. He could talk of God and make Him real because He is real, and Father realized it so fully that the knowledge radiated from him when he spoke of Him. It was good to be born of such a father.

(106)

"How are things going?"

"Pretty good, Father."

"You keep your chin up. Remember that when God loves us, sometimes He lets us suffer for our own good, to detach us from something that is not Himself, or as reparation for our past sins. Our part is to accept these things from His hands gratefully, knowing well that He loves us and knowing that He does not ask any of us to suffer more than He Himself has suffered for our sakes."

"I'm trying to understand that now. I think I am beginning to."

30. Baby Hospital

I ONLY WORKED as a domestic for about one month. Then I went to work at Misericordia, a small Catholic hospital, as a baby nurse. I worked the evening shift from 3 to 11 P.M., and lived in the hospital. On duty I was in charge of a ward that usually held between fifteen and twenty-five babies in good health. I loved them all and spoiled them a little.

At first I was a bit shy, working and living there, because, except for a few patients, I was the only Negro. Most of the nurses were much older than I, but the student nurses and a few of the sisters were very young. If they had been colored, I would have attempted to make friends at once. As it was, I held back.

However, before I had been there a week the student who was in charge of the ward across the hall from me in the evenings came over to talk to me after we had put the lights out for the night and the babies were sleeping. We talked a long time about a lot of things, but that first night most of the conversation was about nursing.

After that when there was a student on duty with me, often she would call me to come to her, or come to me when our wards were quiet and our work completed for a time. We would always leave the door between the wards open, in order that we could hear the faintest call of a patient or cry of an infant. Sometimes the student was a sister, and I think I liked those times best of all.

But whether it was a sister or a regular student on duty, we found that we had many things in common that made conversation not only possible but easy and pleasant. Sometimes at first I felt something like wonder at that— a sort of pleased surprise.

I had never known any white people intimately since I was a tiny girl. As it is in the case of most people, my prejudices were based chiefly on hearsay, and the attitude of these young women and girls completely changed many of my notions.

When we knew each other well enough to discuss this problem of race, I discovered that most of the students felt the same way. They had never known any colored person intimately before they met me. They had been surprised to learn that there was little difference in us besides the color of our skins; that my people lived, loved, worked, planned, dreamed and suffered just as their people; that the same things made us laugh and cry; that there were good and bad among us and that none were *all* good or *all* bad. I think we both felt an uplift in spirit at this discovery. As the months passed we learned to know, respect and like each other.

Sometimes we were serious and sometimes we only laughed and had fun. Often we told each other funny things that had happened to us as we worked in the hospital. Sometimes we helped each other with our work.

One such day, I was fixing the pablum for the babies in the kitchen when a small patient, about six or seven years of age, I guess, came down the hall into the room. He was white; I think all of the patients were white except the maternity cases.

He watched me silently a few moments, then asked, "What you doing?"

"Fixing the babies something to eat."

He was silent again, as if in thought, then asked abruptly, "Nurse, why are you colored?"

I was startled and hardly knew how to answer for a moment. Then I replied, "God made me that way."

"I mean, but were you white at first and then turned that way?"

"No, I was always like this. I have some little colored babies down in the ward, and they are brown already. Would you like to see one of them?"

"Oh, boy!"

"Okay. Come on. You can't come inside now, but you stand right outside the door and I'll bring the little baby there so you can see him."

"All right."

He stared, fascinated, at the brown baby a long time, awed. "Gee," he said at last.

Afterward, when I told the student on duty, we laughed and laughed.

"You think I'm turning?" I asked.

"Not at this late date," she said. "I'm afraid you're stuck."

"You mean no red hair and blue eyes?"

"Uh uh. Nope. You know, maybe we ought to have played a trick on him." And we laughed again.

The sisters at the baby hospital were all French, and some spoke very little English. One such was Sister Alice, who was in charge of the linen for the babies. She had been in the order for forty years. She liked me and used to talk to me a lot, although sometimes we had difficulty understanding each other. Sometimes she would talk to me about my people.

Sometimes she talked to me about God, after she learned

that I liked to speak of Him too. She had several prayer and devotional books which she kept in a drawer in my desk. I used to read them, but since they were all written in French, often I had to ask her to explain a passage which I found difficult to translate. She liked to do that. Her English was bad and my French was worse, but we spoke in the universal language of love when we spoke of Our Lord; where we could find no words, gestures sufficed, so all was well.

She noticed that I went to daily Mass and Holy Communion, and one day asked me why I didn't enter an order and become a nun. I told her why, and she decided that babies were nice to have also and that motherhood was a worthy vocation. She agreed that there is a great need for people willing to live Christian lives in the world, for people who, by their own way of thinking, acting and dealing with others, show forth in practice the tenets of faith and the glory of God in their lives.

She admitted that there is a desperate need for people who, while living in the midst of a society both pagan and skeptical, live with such faith and such charity, such virtue and such hope, that even sinners, skeptics and pagans will have to say of them, as others said of the first Christians, "See how they love one another."

In such an atmosphere as this, prejudice was doomed. I could no longer see these people as "white" but only as "people." In a manner of speaking, I forgot I was colored. I could forget because they could forget.

Then when I went to chapel to Mass in the morning, I lost all my self-consciousness, because I was no longer a stranger to these people, but one with them. It was a wonderful thing to offer again with Christ and all the Christians of the world His perfect sacrifice to His Father.

For the Holy Mass is Calvary again. It is the perfect prayer. We offer good gifts to God, the Father—bread, food of man and reward for his work—wine, fruit of the vine. Christ comes through His priest and becomes our sacrifice—the perfect sacrifice—by making the bread and wine be Himself.

Thus the sacrifice of adoration to God is His Son. When the priest raised Our Lord, that we might adore Him in the Host, I would think that even while we gazed upon Him, we were a part of His Mystical Body, members of Him and of each other.

Then I could understand how He could say that the whole of the law lay in the commandments "Love God" and "Love your neighbor." They were really the same commandment, for neither is possible without the other. Love is the keynote of Christianity; with it, everything is possible, without it, nothing.

I could no longer justify hate nor prejudice against any person, for now I knew my neighbor was anyone whom I could love or serve or who could love or serve me. There's no one else left.

31. For This I Was Born

WHEN DAYS ARE FULL they seem to fly, and my days were very full as a baby nurse. But though I had a lot of pals among the people with whom I lived, sometimes I was lonely. Then it was that I found someone better than a friend, I found a Mother. She had always been my Mother, but I had not always acted like her child, because I had not known her.

I met her quite naturally. Everywhere there is devotion to the Blessed Mother, but perhaps this devotion is most beautifully expressed in a convent, where so many of her daughters, following her example, live to love and serve her Son. There you can often see this devotion in their faces and hear it in their voices. I loved to kneel in the chapel and listen to them as they chanted the prayers aloud in their soft, musical voices. Even on duty sometimes, when the windows were open, I could hear them, since the chapel was directly across from my infants' ward. It was always so beautiful that it made me think, what was she really like, this lady, that she was so beloved of her children? What was she really like who was found worthy to be the Mother of God?

Sister Alice, who spent so many hours with me daily, had a very special devotion to Our Lady. She loved to talk to me about her. So I began to know her, and to know her is to love her.

I knew nothing about meditation as prayer, yet I began to meditate on her life almost daily. When I was caring for the babies I would think of her caring for the Infant Jesus. When they were very cross and trying, and I was tired and growing impatient, I would pretend that I was she and the infant in my arms was the Holy Infant. Then most often I felt my impatience dissolve, and I was ashamed of it. Sometimes I would laugh at myself for my pretense and tell myself to "grow up." But I pretended all the same.

When I made things for my baby, I thought of Our Lady making things for her baby. And always when I became aware of the wonder of the infant stirring in my body, I thought of her wonder at the angel's words, or her happiness when she went to tell her cousin Elizabeth the marvelous thing that had been wrought in her. She too must have felt this wonder at the miracle of life. She must have known this inner secret happiness as she felt her girl's body growing heavy, ripening. She too must have often laughed, a deep low laugh of exultation and delight, when she felt her Baby move within her. Was there any joy or surprise that other mothers know which she had missed? Surely not!

And she had known our sorrows, too. I thought of that when I was unhappy. Distrusted at first even by her spouse, St. Joseph, she had borne it silently and patiently until he could understand. She had been poor and homeless when her child was born. She had had to run away to save her own life and His. She had had to live among strangers in Egypt, and perhaps being a Jew among them was as painful as being a Negro in America sometimes is. She was a real human being, not just a picture saint. She was a mother, and had known all the joys and sorrows of motherhood. How could I ever have thought of her as a stranger? It was nice to meet our Lady Mother in all her love and tenderness. Now I said the rosary not only as an act of faith but also as an act of love.

One morning when I came downstairs from the chapel, I told one of the young sisters whom I liked, "Sister Jean, I'm going to have my baby today."

Sister laughed because she didn't believe me. "Then why don't you report to the hospital?" she teased me.

"I want to finish the sweater for him first. And I want to see if I have any mail." I spoke joyously, so she laughed again and went away, still unconvinced. But I told the truth. My son was born that same afternoon.

I had seen and cared for hundreds of newborn babies, but somehow this was different. This was MY baby, and like any other new mother, I found him strange and wonderful.

I touched one of the too-tiny hands somewhat gingerly, with a curious sense of awe mingled with my happiness. Once, long ago, when I had first come to the hospital to work, and just before that, sometimes in my bitterness or loneliness, I had wondered, "Why was I ever born? Why didn't I die long ago? Why had I lived to suffer and bring forth others from my loins to suffer?"

Now looking back, remembering, I could answer my own questions. I thought of all the things that I had learned in the hospital, of the graces I had received; I thought of the Mother I had found and of the son I had borne who would be her child also. Out of the fullness of my heart, joy overflowed, and I knew that it was for this, for this was I born.

32. House of Hospitality

WHEN McDONALD FRANCIS was two weeks old, we flew home to my mother in Memphis. She was as delighted and as proud of her grandson as I, and loved him as much. Together we cared for him during his first two months. Then I had to go back to New York. I was going back to nursing school later. Meanwhile I had a job in the same hospital where I had worked while waiting for his birth.

Now the days did not fly, but dragged. There was too much free time. Occasionally I went to visit my old classmates at the other hospital, but our lives and interests had grown apart, though we still loved each other. Their conversations about "old times" or other people wearied me. I had no interest in their parties, which I had not attended or could not attend, or in the patients and staff members I didn't know. Often I feigned an interest I didn't feel.

On the other hand, they had no interest in the life of a convent after their first curiosity was sated. And my growing conviction of the necessity of increased Christian consciousness in all our lives, and of the need to baptize a society which was no longer very Christian, frightened them a little.

"You're just overwrought. It's the unnatural environment you live in. A convent! Those sisters are filling you full of religious nonsense. This is 1947. We believe in God and all, but we aren't fanatics about it. The day for that is gone. We've got to be sensible, practical in religion just as in anything else. You've just got to conform to it. You know 'When you are in Rome, do as the Romans do.'"

Such was the attitude of my friends. I understood it very well, since so recently it had been my own. But it was wrong. Now I was beginning to see why it was wrong and where it went wrong, and I couldn't hold to it any more. I knew that as Christians we could not conform to things we knew to be wrong, we had to try to change the world—or as much of it as was in our reach—to a Christian world; we had to at least live our own lives as Christ willed, pleasing to Him, as He had pleased His father. I was confirmed about that time too, and so strengthened in my convictions, and in my faith that through God we can do much more than we think we can.

I tried to fill up this emptiness in my life with movies, concerts, tours of the museums, books, all those things that had once crowded my life till each day was full. But now I could take in all these things and yet an emptiness remained. It was such a huge void, you see, that only God could fill it. So I sought Him. I went to Father Meenan and told him about it.

"That's elegant," he said. "There are some friends of mine I want you to meet. You promised to go last year, then you went to Larchmont instead."

"I remember. I'd like to meet them."

"I'm going down this week. You want to meet me there?"

I did. So he gave me directions to the *Catholic Worker*.

The Catholic Worker movement began in 1933 with Peter Maurin and Dorothy Day, who were convinced, with Pope Leo XIII, that "the Catholic Church, that imperishable handwork of our all-merciful God, has for her immediate and natural purposes the saving of souls and the securing of our happiness in heaven; yet in regard to things temporal she is the source of benefits as manifold and as great as if the chief end of her existence were to insure the prospering of our earthly life." They felt a strong personal responsibility for sharing in the work of restoring all things, temporal as well as spiritual, in Christ.

They started houses of hospitality to provide food, shelter and clothing for the immediate needs of the poor; started round-table discussions for clarification of thought; published leaflets, articles and a monthly newspaper, *The Catholic Worker*. They aimed at forming communes which would become Christian communities of families "where the communal and private aspect of property could be restored and man would receive according to his needs."

Of course, there was much more to it than this, but Father Meenan gave me as much of it as I could absorb at a time. So did the Catholic Workers.

33. Blessed Are the Poor

WHEN I FIRST went down to the *Catholic Worker*, I was struck by the utter poverty in which these people worked and lived, for it was one of the principles of the movement that the Christian must not only alleviate, but also share the poverty of the poor—there in the heart of the slum on Mott Street, just below the Bowery—Chinatown was on one side and the poorest of the Italian immigrant families on the other. A few blocks away the Third Avenue El groaned and screeched.

When I went inside the "office," the plainness of bare walls seemed to me ugly, and so did the beaten old furniture to which some paint still clung despairingly. I was used to the immaculate orderliness of a hospital and was somewhat repelled by the disorderly appearance of the room—papers all over the place, boxes of clothes just received and not yet sorted cluttering the tables, sponges thrown haphazardly over the table. I thought "Somebody ought to clean this up." The workers and the poor who came to them for aid looked just alike, except that the former were a little cleaner, and busy.

A pretty red-haired girl came to meet me at the door, smiling. "Hello, I'm Irene Naughton," she said.

I told her my name, adding, "Father Meenan asked me to come."

She seemed to think very highly of Father Meenan and

she said she was glad I knew him. She told me a lot about the *Catholic Worker*, about the women's house upstairs and the men's house in the back, where they lived with the really destitute, men and women who had nothing and perhaps, having suffered so long, now wanted nothing but what it takes to keep them breathing and moving. She told me about the breadline and clothes room. She gave me some copies of the paper with its cut of a black man and a white one standing together with Our Lord, each with a symbol of work in his hand.

After a while I forgot her plain clothes, and the poor, disordered room, and all its signs of poverty. Or rather those things became the logical background for her and what she said.

Father Meenan came soon and we all had dinner together. There were murals on the walls of the dining room, showing Christ, The Worker. He looked thin and spent and poor like these people, as if someone had told Him, too, "You can't change the world," and He was still trying.

I didn't stay long that day, but I came again and again after that. Soon, in fact, almost all my time off duty, except when I was in Church or asleep, was spent there.

I met Dorothy Day and Peter Maurin—though Peter was sick even then, and I couldn't talk to him—who started the movement for love of God and their brothers in Him. I met gentle Jack English, who took care of the kitchen and cooking and (I always thought) did a lot to hold hot tempers checked. I met Dave Mason, who is big and jolly and always made me think of Santa Claus, but who can think and write so clearly about the evils of a society which has grown away from God and our need to go back to Him. And Tom Sullivan, who has an

Irish temper but knows how to feel the tragedy of Mott Street in the people who live there and yet sees the beauty of another kind of poverty for love of God. And Bob Ludlow, who wrote of pacifism, and who, I was sure, only God could have made a pacifist, for he seemed more like one of those revolutionaries who sacrifice everything for the Ideal, at last even the Ideal itself, and leave their footprints in the sands of time in blood.

At first, though, I was not sure I even liked the *Catholic Worker*, especially after I started going down there every day. The people, the place, the ideal were so very different from anything that I had ever known. They said that the world's chaos was born when Christians forgot the implications of the teachings of Christ, forgot that "Christian" meant "follower of Christ," when Catholics forgot the spiritual and social doctrines of the Church. They said the world was sick, and they claimed they had the remedy and lived as if they had. Yet they were neither smug nor complacent. There seemed in each of them a great compassion and in most a great humility. It was this, I think, that I couldn't understand—how they could be so sure and yet stay humble. But then, my ideas on humility had to undergo a great change too.

I didn't understand how they could take the abuse and curses of those men and women who benefited from their hospitality, who ate their food and wore their clothes and slept in their beds and gave nothing in return, not even "thank you." I didn't understand how they could be so enthused over homemade bread and beef stew when dinner time came. I didn't understand how they could get up in the morning, wash in cold water or a cold room, dress in somebody's hand-me-down clothes, and rush off to Mass and tell God thanks, in all sincerity, for that. I didn't understand the violence and bitterness they inspired in some others, including some of my Catholic friends. What were they doing after all, and who were they? A group of poor people, living among the poor, speaking and writing of the love of God in Himself and in each other. What was there so special about this way of life that one must either follow it or fight it, that one must either love or despise? Why could one not remain indifferent?

Then there were times when I did not think some of them were humble in some things, particularly in regard to art and books. There seemed to be intolerance here that bordered on intellectual pride. There seemed too great a readiness to laugh at something one didn't like.

Part of this may have been due to my own injured pride. I remember one day in particular when I was in the back office working on the files. Bob was sitting behind me at his desk, talking to someone (I don't remember who). Earlier I had been showing Dorothy some poems I had written (I fancied myself a poet in those days), and she had read them and put them on his desk. He picked one up and read it, then another. He put both down on the desk.

"That's horrible," he said. "Who wrote this stuff? It sounds like something from Edgar Guest!"

I was very still, and hoped that my name was not on it. I had no desire to defend my work (which was probably just as well).

After I knew them better I learned that the thing that made these people so special, and their way of life so strange and compelling—or repulsive, depending on which group you were in, that of friend or that of enemy —was the fact that here were very ordinary people who had found a great truth and were trying to live according to it. Their discovery had revolutionized their own lives, as well as the lives of a lot of other people, and aimed at revolutionizing the whole of society, but it had not taken from them any of their own humanity. It had not made them angels. They were trying to be saints, but in their own human bodies, with their own human wills, subject to imperfections. Which is as it should be. But it meant that they were subject to failure, like others. It meant that not every action would seem that of a saint. That didn't take away, however, from the worth of the truth they had found.

I think it was these things that so many of their critics, such as my Catholic friends before mentioned, did not understand.

After a while, I understood that these people had felt the emptiness and hunger that were a part of my life now, and learned the secret of filling it. I went to them to learn the secret. In all their poverty they were richer than I—and I knew I wanted to be poor—as they were poor.

34. Neither Communism Nor Capitalism

Soon they let me do odd jobs around the *Worker*, things that everybody else was too busy to do or which freed someone for something more important which I could not do. Sometimes I kept the clothes room for Irene or answered letters. Sometimes I helped John Paul, one of the men who lived there, clean up the office. Rarely, I helped peel potatoes. Mostly I did the carding and helped Charlie O'Rourke (one of the workers—tall, thin, immaculate, looking for all the world like a movie "editor") keep the files straight. Once I messed them up for him. He was annoyed at first, then he showed me the right way to do it. There was so much work and so few to take the responsibility; often I'd think of our Lord's words, "The harvest indeed is great, but laborers are few; pray ye therefore to the Lord of the harvest that He send laborers into his fields."

Some of the things I learned from them were easy to understand and accept, others were harder. I could understand voluntary poverty and a house of hospitality where the involuntarily poor could come for food, clothing and shelter. I could understand the mystical insight into man as one in whom we served and loved Christ, serving and loving him. I could accept the farm with its retreat house, where conferences were held to nourish and feed the hunger for God by the words of God. I understood daily Mass and reception of the Food of the Eucharist and the snatched hours or minutes spent before the tabernacle in worship, praise and adoration as much as supplication. I could understand community work and prayer as an essential part of community living.

But I didn't see what these things had to do with pacifism, or non-violent resistance. I hated war, not as a moral but as a human evil; because it hurt, not because it offended God. Yet I thought it was often the only possible solution to national differences; I did not trust the efficacy of merely spiritual weapons like works and prayers, especially when the other fellow was using bombs and guns. I guess I imagined somehow that the latter were the more powerful—imagined our weapons stronger than God's!

I did not understand what all this had to do with capitalism—"certainly it's communism we're fighting? Is one not the opposite of the other?" I did not see that our choice lay beyond either of these, and so the aim to "establish a society which provides for the necessities of all, where needs determine production and labor would receive the full equivalent of goods produced" sounded to me distressingly like the ideal of that Godless philosophy which we fought and must fight as Christians. That worried me until I began to read more of Peter Maurin's writings. One essay seemed particularly helpful in clearing this up for me:

"Christianity has nothing to do with either modern capitalism or modern communism, for Christianity has a capitalism of its own and a communism of its own.

"Modern capitalism is based on property without

responsibility, while Christian capitalism is based on property with responsibility.

"Modern communism is based on poverty through force. For a Christian, voluntary poverty is the ideal, as exemplified by St. Francis of Assisi, while private property is not an absolute right but a gift which, as such, cannot be wasted but must be administered for the benefit of God's children."

That, and simply living with Dorothy, hearing her speak and seeing how she put what she said into action. (That's something you don't quite get, usually, from just hearing her lecture or reading what she says.) There is a warmness about her, a tenderness—woman, mother. You sense that in her when she is talking about the children of the poor or the Negro. There is not a looking down, there is a lifting up and sharing, a unity.

She really cares that Kay's baby is sick, that Margaret didn't come in and is probably drunk some place, that there is dissension at the farm in Newburgh, that there is a race riot in Palisades, that Christians are going to be drafted to kill each other for non-Christian states, in non-Christian combat for non-Christian ideals. She really sees in this insolent beggar, smelling of whiskey, the Person of Christ. She sees in this brown girl His sister—nay, more, a member of His Mystical Body.

After I grew to know her better, I began trying to see things through her eyes. They looked a lot different then.

35. The Retreat

ONE DAY when I was down at the *Catholic Worker*, Irene told me about a women's retreat in New Kingston, Pennsylvania, conducted by the Apostolate of Mary. Dorothy said if I wanted to go, I could drive down with two of her friends from Kentucky who were going. Both were white. One was, like me, a student nurse, so we would probably have much in common, Dorothy said. At the *Catholic Worker* I had now become myself and grown used to meeting others who were "color blind," so I did not hesitate to go with them but was glad. They were both very friendly from the first, and we found conversation easy despite our racial differences. That was one of the things we talked about on our way to New Kingston—racial differences and the racial problem.

"There is something different and special about all peoples, races," said Mary. "You people, for instance, can feel things, have a sort of gentleness, and an understanding kind of tenderness, and you know how to laugh."

"Yet it's these differences—that God meant to be good—that make us hate each other," said Alice. "We decide some accidental qualities are superior qualities, so we have 'inferior' and 'superior' races."

"As children we accept the imaginary fact of our superiority," Mary explained, "because that is what we are taught. That is how everyone is around you, people you respect. I was like that myself until I realized the meaning of the Church. If we are one body in Christ and both receiving and being nourished by His real Body in the Eucharist, we can't hate each other, because we are a part of each other. Through reading and talking to some other people I began to understand that, and knew I couldn't stay prejudiced and be really Catholic. So I began to try to understand your people."

I said that my experience had been a similar one of conversion from hate and distrust to love.

At last we reached the retreat house. There were about fifteen retreatants. We read the rules the first afternoon; the retreat didn't begin until night. There was to be silence throughout, including the periods of work and recreation.

In the morning there would be meditation in the chapel, then we sang the Mass of the Angels. Then the Angelus, followed by breakfast. After that were the conferences, about three or four a day, each followed by fifteen minutes of prayer before the Blessed Sacrament. Between these periods, we did our assigned housework. Everyone had some job to do.

During recreation, we could walk around the grounds or to the corner, or sit on the beautiful porch or in chapel, thinking and praying.

There was time in the warm, friendly silence that had settled over the retreat house like a blanket, to see ourselves and our faults, our needs and desires in the light of Christian perfection. There was time to make serious resolutions for amendment and improvement. And I think we all did these things.

Yet the week was not without laughter or joy. I don't

know why it is, but many, if not most, people seem to think that the struggle for Christian perfection, that is, living in accord with the teachings of Christ, takes all the joy out of life; that it is necessarily a dull, monotonous, dreary existence, without laughter, without smiles; a long-faced, gray existence without any beauty at all. That's simply not true. The Christian way does not take joy and laughter from our lives, but puts them there. It gives back the clean, fresh joys and purity and the innocent laughter of children. That's why Paul could say, "Rejoice always," and Our Lord could say, " . . . that my joy may be in them, and their joy may be full."

The Christian who can find nothing to laugh at had better re-examine his concept of Christianity; there is probably something very wrong with it. Humility is the beginning of charity and sanctity, but the ability to laugh at ourselves, even our problems and mistakes, is the beginning of humility. There can be no bitterness nor despair where there is laughter.

When the silent week came to an end, talking, which had once seemed so necessary, at first seemed strange and superfluous, and we found ourselves sometimes whispering unnecessarily. Going back home and saying goodbye to people with whom I had lived but a week and spoken to only once or twice was surprisingly painful. But it was time to go and try to practice some of the things which I had learned.

I needed someone to guide me, though, and my friend Father Meenan had left the city and been given a post at the seminary in Norwalk, Connecticut. So I went to Father Kirby, another priest in the same parish, whom I had known a long time and liked very much. He was very different from Father Meenan, though I find it hard to explain their differences.

Father Meenan was a thinker whose depth of thought is caught up and half concealed by a keen sense of humor and matter-of-fact logic. He will say with good-humored candor, "Thank God for all those things that make you suffer, for all your trials and hardships . . . Grace is purchased by sanctity and sanctity by suffering." He will smile then, as if to say, "and that's that."

Father Kirby is little and a bit shy. He will say, "Love is the secret of sanctity. Love ardently and be obedient . . . to accept the ordinary, humble path as our way to God . . . that is the 'little way,'" and then he will seem a bit embarrassed at being given the keeping of so big a secret, and being allowed to share it.

36. "Forgive Us Our Trespasses"

AFTER I RETURNED to work in New York City, I was increasingly troubled by an old problem. Up to that time I had been fairly successful in pushing it to the back of my mind and ignoring it, but I found this more and more difficult to do. I had made one decision and considered it final; now reluctantly I questioned the justice and mostly the charity of it.

Some weeks before, I had received a letter which had been the starting point of it all.

"I know that I have made a mistake," it read, "but I am sorry and I want to make up for this, if you will forgive me. After all, Butch needs his father too, and I think I can be a good father.

"Now I know what you mean by God. You will be happy to know I am being baptized, too, whether you change your mind about me or not."

There was more of this. I didn't want to read it and I didn't answer it. I told myself that that was all over, and better so.

Yet now my conscience reproached me. I knew that if he had sinned against me, we both had in many ways sinned against God. If he needed my forgiveness, we both needed His. Could I expect forgiveness, if I would not forgive?

I gave myself many sensible, logical and entirely

practical reasons for holding to my first decision. Forgiveness is certainly good, and so is forgetfulness—up to a point; but what was it that my father used to say? "If a man deceive me once, shame on him; if he deceive me twice, shame on me." Wasn't that a good philosophy? Wouldn't any sensible person agree with it? Or did forgiveness necessarily imply forgetting and giving a new chance? When charity quarreled with prudence or reason, which were we to consider? I remembered the gospel in which one of His disciples prudently asked Jesus, "How many times shall my brother offend me and I forgive him—till seven times?"

But Our Lord answered him, "I say to thee, not till seven times but till seventy times seven."

But perhaps this was different. I looked for excuses and found none. And every morning at Mass, when I received Holy Communion, Our Lord seemed to reproach me. I was more than ever conscious of my own offenses against Him.

All the time that this battle raged within me I still carried on my work as before; mornings at *The Worker*, evenings on duty at the hospital. I was learning a lot in those mornings about patience and forgiveness and second chances too. There was so much suffering there, mental and physical, so many crosses of ingratitude, enmity, and spitefulness to be borne, and these from people who should have been friends. Yet there was joy, and hope against hope. There were countless failures, yet no despair; they kept trying.

There were people who came to them for love, food, shelter, sympathy and encouragement and in return gave mockery, ingratitude and occasionally even violence.

Time after time I saw patience and forgiveness extend

far beyond reasonable limits. But with these, it was not a question of whether forgiveness was reasonable or deserved but whether or not it was what Our Lord would have done.

All right. So this woman came in drunk and cursing in the middle of the night, disturbing everyone, scandalizing the neighbors, picking a quarrel with other women in the house, being sick on the floor. She was still poor and homeless. She needed shelter, and this was all she had. But Christ was in her and she was undoubtedly pitied and loved by Him. For His sake we must try to love her, to help her and forgive her. We must pray for her.

Or maybe it was a man, shoeless and coatless, who came begging in the deepest winter, only to sell what they gave him on the Bowery and spend the money on a bottle of cheap liquor. Drunk, and sometimes profane, he would come back still looking for a coat, almost demanding it as a right. You couldn't send him out to freeze or catch pneumonia—that is, not if you had a coat and shoes to give him. If there were no more in the clothing room, maybe there was an extra one in your scanty wardrobe, so you gave that.

Very impractical, you think? People ought to be allowed to profit from their mistakes, not be encouraged in them. But bad people, careless, thoughtless, uncaring people also get hungry and cold. They also starve and freeze. They also belong to God. It takes great faith and charity to see that, and to go on forgiving and helping, to go on offering other chances even in the face of continued failure. But I saw such forgiveness and help extended day after day.

Then I knew that I would have to forgive also. I could

no longer deceive myself. Forgiveness is as much a part of Christianity as being sorry. Even when I prayed, I said, "Forgive as we forgive." If I wanted forgiveness of God, I must forgive; if I wanted His mercy, I must be merciful. So I answered the letter.

"I am glad that you have 'found God.' And I do forgive you. The past is dead, we won't think or speak of it again. As for the future, we will speak of that when you come back." As I sealed it, I smiled a little wryly and thought, "Forgive us our trespasses as we forgive those who trespass against us—and help us to forgive those who trespass against us."

37. West Meets East

THE MESSAGE OF Fatima, where Our Lady appeared in Portugal and promised the conversion of Russia if people prayed and did penance, had given me a deep interest in and curiosity concerning the Russian people. So I was very pleased one day when a young woman who was visiting *The Catholic Worker* told me that she was going to a Catholic church where the ceremonies were in the tradition of the ancient Eastern church instead of the Roman tradition. I was a little doubtful at first, because I knew nothing of the Eastern churches, to which many Russian and Slavic peoples belong. However, since I had confidence in my friend, I promised to meet her the following Sunday. Meanwhile I wanted to learn as much about the Eastern churches as possible.

I believe it was she who suggested that I read Donald Attwater's book, *The Catholic Eastern Churches*, which explains that they are Catholic, one in faith and under the jurisdiction of the Pope and the Holy See. I learned that the Mass, which they call the Divine Liturgy, is said in many languages besides Latin, and that the forms themselves differ. These and the other things which I learned fed my eagerness to go to St. Michael's, and I could hardly wait for Sunday to come.

Trying to describe St. Michael's is like trying to describe a person with a strong and endearing personality, and all words seem pitifully inadequate. Yet I will try.

First, it is a plain red brick building with heavy iron doors. You would never suppose that it was a church unless someone told you or you noticed the small sign "St. Michael's Chapel."

Inside there is a small hallway with steps leading upstairs and another door leading into the chapel itself. The chapel looks somewhat like the illustrations in Attwater's book, only not so rich, for it is a poor little chapel. There are the Holy Doors and the ikons, beautiful painted pictures of Our Lord and Lady. The center door of the "Great Entrance" has curtains which are closed during parts of the celebration of the Divine Liturgy. There are no more than one or two folding chairs, for the whole congregation stands except the old, the sick or the women with babies.

Upstairs is a small kitchenette and a dining room. Most of the congregation, and the choir and the priest come here before and after Mass to drink coffee and eat queer delicious breads. This is where everyone becomes acquainted—you introduce yourself or are introduced.

Those who come often and regularly are eventually assigned to kitchen duty in groups of three or four. They are the ones who make the coffee and slice the bread. They keep the cups and the tables filled. The others sit and talk and talk. Ideas and views are exchanged. The latest news, books or scientific discovery are discussed from a Christian viewpoint. Here there is no trace of racial or social consciousness or superiority. Here Christian meets Christian in such evident brotherhood that the stranger must say, "See how they love one another."

But no one can remain a stranger long, unless he wishes it himself. The welcome is too warm for that. More beautiful and marvelous even than this spirit of Christian brotherhood that pervades the place like a sweet odor, is the Divine Liturgy itself. It is always sung in Slavonic.

We were a little late, and the choir was already singing the responses of the Great Litany.

"*For the peace of the whole world, for the welfare of God's Holy Churches and for the union of them all, let us pray to the Lord.*"

"*Lord have mercy.*"

This fervent cry for peace rings throughout the entire liturgy. "*For the whole world—peaceful times—for a day all-perfect, holy, peaceful and sinless—for the angel of peace . . .*"—always the cry for peace.

I thought of all that I had heard of the Russian people. This did not fit with those things. This was their liturgy. Could so many have forgotten it? Or was it perhaps this very cry that had won for them the intercession of Our Lady of Fatima?

At the solemn moment when the bread and the wine we had offered were to become the Body and Blood of Christ, all of us except the choir knelt on the bare, polished wooden floors; before, the hosannas had been sung loudly and joyfully; now all was silent except for the priest's voice coming to us from behind the drawn curtain.

Then the priest intoned, "*Thine own of Thine own we offer Thee . . .*"

And the choir responded, "*We praise Thee, we bless Thee, we give Thee thanks . . .*"

Then followed another litany for pardon, peace, unity, for "*all that is good and profitable for our souls*" and for a good defense before the dread judgment of Christ.

Finally, there was the Communion, with the preceding

prayer, "*I believe . . . that Thou art . . . the Christ, the son of the Living God Who did come into the world to save sinners, of whom I am the chief . . .*"

"To save sinners of whom I am the chief." It was true; never had I been so conscious of my own unworthiness, as I approached the priest to receive the Bread of Life.

"I believe that This is Thy Sacred Body and This Thy Precious Blood . . ."

For the first time I received Holy Communion under the two forms of bread and wine.

Following the Communion were alleluias and the closing prayers. At the end, in English, was a prayer for Russia, then everyone began leaving—most went upstairs; so did we.

But there and outside, later, and even on duty that afternoon, I was filled with the remembrance of its beauty. I knew I would go back, as I thought of the richness, the depth, the beauty and fullness of our faith. Now I understand why we say the Church is universal.

I went back again and again and loved it more each time.

I made friends, too, especially with Gail Malley and Helen Dolan. Like me, they were of the Western (Roman) rite, but like me, they loved the Eastern rite at St. Michael's. They came every Sunday, and at last Gail and I decided to join the choir. As I remember it, it was Gail's idea at first, but I was just as enthusiastic about it when she suggested it as I could have been if I had thought up the idea myself.

We had to learn the alphabet before we could even read the words, never mind pronounce them, but everybody helped us and it went pretty fast. After we began to learn it, we loved it more than ever. The words and

(*138*)

the music of the chant and songs were so beautiful that we practiced anywhere. We even sang parts from the Divine Liturgy aloud together on the subway on our way home, or when going some place together. Gail sang alto and I sang soprano then, so we sang in harmony. At first, the people would stare, but as we ignored their stares and continued singing, they almost always began to smile—friendly, understanding, tolerant smiles. Some even seemed a bit envious of that we had together. For all, though, it must have seemed strange, perhaps to many a wonderful, impossible thing, to see a white girl and a colored girl singing something like Russian together aloud on a New York subway. Strange or not, it made us happy; it made them smile; and God was praised; so I guess it was a good thing.

Helen was a little older than we were, but it didn't seem to matter. Queer, but this Christian ideal of friendship for Christ's sake is a lot different even in the simplest things from the friendships the world knows without Him. Incidentals like color, age and race have a disconcerting way of disappearing altogether or becoming almost meaningless. Helen was the one who treated us to sodas and movies, because Gail and I both went to school and were always "financially embarrassed." And she never seemed to mind this one-sided affair; on the contrary, she shared gladly with us what she had of the world's goods.

38. "Your X-ray Is Questionable"

SUMMER PASSED and winter came, and I was supposed to re-enter nursing school in December. I was not going back to the school at Harlem Hospital, but the superintendent of nurses, Mrs. Daley, had made it possible for me to enter another school in Brooklyn with full credit for all the work which I had already completed. I almost didn't want to go back, because it seemed to me that the things which I was now doing and learning were more important. Yet, since I had started, I wanted to finish. It was even possible that I might do more good as a registered nurse than as a baby nurse, so I was going back. When the time did come at last, I said goodbye with difficulty. The babies, the sisters, and especially the chapel were dear to me. Too dear, perhaps. But on December 17th I took my final leave and entered the new hospital as a student.

I had been ill for about a week or more with a "cold," and when I went on duty one day, I still had a cough. I worked several days, and then had to report to the infirmary for an X-ray and physical examination.

The day following, the superintendent of nurses called me and told me, as gently as possible, "Your X-ray is questionable. There is a possibility that you have a beginning tubercular process in your lungs."

I was shocked but not afraid. My knowledge of tuberculosis was very vague and general, little more, actually, than a layman's. But I was worried about my mother. She would be terribly upset. And Butch—I waited for the nurse to continue.

"We are not positive, but we want to make certain. We want you to go out for a few weeks and take it easy. You don't have to stay in bed or anything like that, but try to rest. We will have you examined by our best specialist, and if there is anything wrong they will find it, so don't worry about it."

I explained to her that I had no family in the city, only friends. She asked if it would be possible for me to stay with some of them until they decided what was to be done with me. Immediately I thought of my friends at *The Catholic Worker*, and I said I thought so. She said that would be fine. So later that evening I moved to *The Worker*.

Weeks passed, and still there was no word from the hospital, no further X-rays, no physical examinations, and I still hadn't told my mother. She believed that I was well and in school. I did not want to worry her until I was absolutely certain, but I was getting very impatient waiting. I didn't know what to do. I wasn't even certain whether I ought to stay in bed or not.

Christmas came and went, and January rolled in, with still no word from the hospital. So my friends decided for me. I was to rest in bed until I learned something definite, and if that wasn't soon, they would send me to a doctor who could prescribe further treatment.

At last I did go to him, and he examined me and said that he found no disease. When I told him about the questionable X-ray of December, he said he would check the old one and take a new one and see what the truth was.

Meanwhile these and all the many difficulties of trying

to go back to nursing school, together with my love for the work which I had been doing and the half-formed desire to live, as fully as my responsibilities as a mother would allow, in accord with the practices as well as the teachings of *The Catholic Worker* had quite taken the edge off my desire to go back to nursing school.

I was willing to give it up but not certain that it was the best thing. I asked my friend and adviser, Father Kirby, if he thought all these difficulties might be meant to show me that it was not God's will for me to be a nurse, that my vocation might lie elsewhere. He answered that such a thing was possible, but that sometimes Our Lord wants us to overcome difficulties and obstacles that lie in the path of what He wants us to become. But he left the decision for me to make, advising me to pray that God's will be done in me, and that I have the courage to accept it humbly.

The very next day I was given another X-ray and it was developed at once, with the verdict "non-tubercular." I breathed a sigh of joy and relief even as the doctor went on to say that he still thought it best that I rest a few months—just in case.

I called the hospital and told the superintendent of nurses all that he had said, and asked for permission to go away for a few weeks to *The Catholic Worker* farm in Newburgh, New York. She replied that the doctors appointed by the city would have to decide my case and that she could do nothing. Completely dejected, and mentally exhausted, I hung up the receiver and returned to my bed. I tried to say, as Father Kirby had bidden me, "Thy will be done," but the words sounded strange, and I did not believe I meant them from my heart, so I said instead, "Make me want Your will and not my own."

However, a few days later I was called to the hospital, given a patch test, and told to return for reading in forty-eight hours. I did. And when I returned the infirmary nurse glanced at my arm and told me to be in the hospital by ten o'clock that night, prepared to go on duty at eight o'clock the next morning.

I was so astounded by the suddenness and unexpectedness of it, that I was almost speechless. Finally I managed to ask for a few days to get ready, but she said, "You'd better do as you are told."

So that was that. At ten o'clock, I was in the hospital, at eight o'clock the next morning I was on duty.

39. Indifference and Efficiency

THE NEW HOSPITAL was not at all like the others. The school especially was different, with a subtle difference that for a long time escaped me. Then one day I knew what it was. There was no school spirit or nursing spirit. Excepting the seniors, my "big sister" class, most of the students seemed to regard nursing merely as a career, a very fine career, no doubt, but nothing more.

They were not bad or careless nurses, just mediocre and indifferent. Even among ourselves in student association and club meetings, this indifference prevailed. Motions were carried almost unanimously, not because everyone agreed, but because no one cared enough to argue. They were not interested in discussing the serious news and problems of the day, such as war, communism or socialized medicine. Thinking was strictly for the classroom and maybe the ward. Discussion of religion, philosophy or race embarrassed them, especially the latter problem when the group was a mixture of white and colored students.

The latest song or movie hit, the current "best seller," the latest and juiciest morsel of gossip about someone we knew, the private lives of movie stars or other "greats," these things decided the conversation. Or sometimes it was men, in general and particular. Everyone was an authority on that subject.

They made me remember my high school days. Then I had been enthralled by such conversations. Now I thought them silly and childish. A day in the students' sitting room might turn up a conversation like this (any day):

"Did you see that new interne?"

"Is he something! I could go for him myself."

"They say he's engaged, wonder if he is?"

"There is many a slip 'tween the cup and the lip. Let her worry about that."

"He's rough, though, reminds me of James Mason."

"Gee that's a guy for you. Give them to me rough. Did you see *The Seventh Veil?*"

"Wasn't that something? When he hit her!"

"Woo woo!"

"You going out tonight?"

"Unless the place falls in or one of us breaks a leg. Jack's taking me to the 'Latin Quarter.'"

"I like it there but I've only been once. We go to the 'Zanzibar.'"

"That's colored, isn't it?"

"Yes, but a lot of colored go to the 'Latin Quarter.'"

"I know. Who's going to get the tickets tonight?"

"What tickets?"

"To the academy of music." (Scornful laughter.) "Yehudi Menuhin is playing."

"Give me Billy Ekstein."

"Wonder if anyone is going?"

"Oh, probably, Adams, Butcavage or some of that bunch."

"Or that new girl, Caldwell."

"Yeah. Give me something down to earth that I can understand. Never mind all that hoty toty stuff."

"Hey, why doesn't someone turn on the radio?"

"Oh, there's nothing on but news. Don't you get sick of news?"

"Don't know, never listen to it. Give me something pleasant."

"Don't you love Lux Radio Theatre?"

"Um humn, and Arthur Godfrey."

"Say who's on duty tonight?"

"I am, worse luck, and we've got a patient there's a pip! She wants a drink of fresh water. She wants her back rubbed. She wants something to make her sleep. And if you don't pay any attention to her, she's ready to report you to the supervisor when she makes rounds."

"Don't you hate patients like that? We have one on our ward. She is a Porto Rican, doesn't understand hardly a word of English, and she is always crying, '*Dolor, dolor, O mama mia, Santa Maria!*'* She's always wanting attention."

"I'll sure be glad when I graduate. This is killing me."

"I know what you mean. I've got to go; if I'm not dressed you know how Jack is."

"Don't I know it? Mike is the same way."

"See you later."

"Okay."

Again and again I reminded myself that most of these girls were just out of high school and had never had any responsibilities to make them grow up. But I could not forget that to them were entrusted daily the bodies, and to a certain extent even the souls, of men, women and children who would have only what they gave. A broken body needs the tenderest, most skillful nursing care, but a broken soul must be handled even more delicately.

* "Pain, pain, O mother, Holy Mary!"

Only a close following of the Great Physician can insure its healing. If one has no high regard for Him, how can His orders be accomplished?

Carelessness, inefficiency, ignorance, even real corruption can be fought openly, because they are obvious, but mediocrity and indifference are more subtle. But they are not lesser evils for that. As the Holy Scriptures say: "But because thou art lukewarm and neither cold nor hot, I will begin to vomit thee out of my mouth." So I feared and hated these more than real corruption, because they are more difficult to fight and more contagious.

The attitudes on many of the wards were little different. "Good nursing care" meant "efficient nursing care." It meant giving the patient the acme of physical comfort and care, medications and treatments exactly on time, food prepared and served well, temperatures taken and recorded accurately, and all charting and other records kept exactly. Every nurse and patient will admit that these things are very important, but are they all-important? Are they the only important things?

Are we not concerned with the mental and spiritual welfare of our patients? If it takes a little more time to listen to Mrs. Smith's long-drawn-out tale of her marital problems and Johnny's wildness, shall we make expediency and efficiency our first consideration? Or shall we take the time to listen, sympathize, console and advise— and make up for it somewhere else? The hospital rules say that the priest must be called for all Catholic patients who are critically ill. Does that mean, then, that we must not bother to ask those less seriously ill if they would like to see the priest or their minister?

A nurse is given unparalleled opportunity for doing

the corporal and spiritual works of mercy, and bound to do so by the pledge which she takes. Deliberately to neglect this duty, then, is a grave fault and an ugly stain on the purity of her pledge and the purity of her soul.

40. Growing Up

I REMEMBER one efficiency record that I received as I left one service. It said in effect: "Miss Caldwell is an average student. However, she lacks poise and must be consistently supervised. She seems to be more concerned with the spiritual welfare of her patients than with their nursing care."

When I read it, I was very angry, because almost my entire period of time on that service was spent working evenings and alone, with no supervision, without even assistance. Even the statement regarding my "greater concern for the spiritual welfare" of my patients hurt and angered me at first. But when I told a friend at St. Michael's about it, she was delighted and expected me to be delighted also.

"What a beautiful thing to have said about you!" she rejoiced.

I had not thought about it in that way before, but now I knew that it was. Although it was not true, it should have been true. The soul is immeasurably more precious than the body and should be more highly regarded. But I had fallen into the error of the spirit of the age which holds spiritual values inferior to material progress and efficiency and humanitarianism, and so I had been hurt. Now I was fiercely glad of the accusation.

There were other things which were sometimes annoying and sometimes amusing. Some of my schoolmates considered daily Mass and silent grace before meals the most blatant hypocrisy. And when my "big sisters" and I discussed religion and life, often they would stare at me with an amazed incredulity. The expressed desire to live by faith is shocking in this sophisticated age of reason.

One day I was coming off duty for supper and found a group of students standing in the hall before my door while one peeked in the keyhole.

"Are you looking for me?" I asked as calmly as I could.

They turned as one to regard me with shocked dismay and began to make excuses and apologies. I disregarded them and walked into my room, closed the door behind me and hung a towel over it. I sat down on my bed, not knowing whether to laugh or cry.

What did it mean anyway? Was I to have no privacy or freedom? Was there something wrong about wanting to live for God? Or was there no room for God here?

What had they expected to see, anyhow? Obviously, they had believed that I was in my room. What had they expected to find me doing; what secret life did they suppose I lived? Had they expected to find me beating myself with cords or prostrate before some image? I was no Margaret of Cortona, seeking out great penances —not even the relatively small penance of having my smallest actions subject to unsympathetic, perhaps scornful and mocking observation. I was sorry for my sins of the past, but I did not worry about them and was content to leave them in the past and try to avoid them in the present. I wanted to be left in peace and treated just like everybody else. I didn't want them to notice me, nor comment especially on my actions.

But such peace and such anonymity seemed impossible to me here. Perhaps they are for a Christian anywhere, because in every man Christ wants to be born, and in the Christian He is, but the struggles of the labor are shocking and repulsive to those who do not understand the birth or know what it is.

Suddenly I remembered a story about a man and a woman. They were far away from home, and the woman carried under her heart an Infant who wanted to be born in the hearts of men and into the world. And they searched for a place where she might bring Him forth—for there was no room for them at the inn. No room at all.

It was hard then to see in the Infant Christ, God, the Lord of Heaven and earth. It is harder still to see Him in the first stirrings of the Christ-life in us. Our Lord says we must be born again, and the soul newborn in Grace is awkward and clumsy, as the newborn are.

If I had been a more perfect Christian, or one farther still away from Grace, I might have attracted less notice than I did, but because I was still an infant in this I attracted much notice from critical observers and skeptics. If I had loved God less or more, I might have won much more of their understanding and sympathy; but as it was, they were shocked, scornful or incredulous. In the Christ-life I was an infant, and they were impatient of my awkward, clumsy efforts. I did not know any of this, of course, so I could not understand it.

When a baby learns to crawl, it seems to him a great achievement and quite a satisfactory means of locomotion. It is only to the onlookers that it seems painful and clumsy. The sentimental mother, unable to watch the awkward struggle, may even pick him up lest he hurt himself. But the wise mother interferes only when he is in real danger. She knows it is natural and necessary to growth.

When we are born again in Christ, we are as infants and we must go through all these awkward and painful processes that are part of "growing up." At first Our Lord carries us tenderly in His arms, as a mother carries her infant; but the time comes when He lets us crawl, that we may learn to stand and walk alone, assisted only by grace. He is always near, as the mother is always near, but unseen.

Our families, friends and even we ourselves see only the visible part of this process, the clumsy, awkward part, and are afraid, not understanding. Everything has been so smooth, placid, normal; now suddenly the whole world is turned upside down.

Once you were certain of what you were and what you wanted, but now you aren't so sure. Once you wanted admiration, position, comfort, luxury; you wanted the whole world at your feet and your own happiness first, last and always. Now you are afraid of all those things. You haven't learned yet to choose from them those things which may be perfected by grace and used for God's glory, and to reject the rest. So you want to reject them all. You have begun to crawl.

My friends were puzzled. Something was happening to me, and they could not understand. I was not the same girl who had gone to school with them and been outstanding in my class. I was not the vain, ambitious girl who had wanted what she wanted when she wanted it, and never mind the rest of the world. Who was this self-conscious, awkward, clumsy creature, always on the defensive? Who was not content to leave religion where it properly belonged—in the church—but who would intrude it into daily life? And what was she defending? A "queer," unheard-of, fanatical idea of personal responsibility in God for all men.

In classes we had studied the human mind and learned a lot about complexes and overcompensation. Surely this was a case of overcompensation with a possible guilt complex behind it. I had been hurt; now I was afraid to face reality and attempting to escape in the supernatural, in what I called God. Such things as these they said among themselves, and they pitied me.

But harder to bear than their attitude toward me, was my attitude toward myself, for I agreed. I thought I was losing my reason; and I was afraid with a terrible fear. I was even afraid to tell anyone of my fear for a long time, though finally I did nerve myself to tell my friend Father Kirby. He tried to reassure me, but in vain.

"Father, I am having so much more difficulty in adjusting to the new school than I did the first time. Do you think it is me?"

"It could be, of course. What sort of difficulties?"

I told him some of them, including the incident at the door of my room. "They were actually looking through the keyhole," I finished. "What do you think they were expecting to see?"

I think he smiled a little. In fact, now that it was past, as I remembered it, I could not help smiling a little myself.

"I know that sort of thing is difficult," he said, "but the fact that you meet these difficulties should not disquiet you. You want really to serve God in God's own way. Do not be surprised that your very efforts to be pure, obedient, etc., should be the cause of suspicion. Other people who are necessarily outside our own mind attribute some ulterior motive to our activity. Love of God, sure, but only that, never. The reason is this, that we are so human that all we do has a human touch."

"But do you think I'm going overboard?"

"No, you aren't doing anything to worry about. Just

stay obedient, and trust in Our Lord. All of this fits into the Divine plan. Suppose nobody opposed us, nobody doubted our ability, nobody objected to a thing we did. Progress? Plenty—but for whose sake? We would soon be buried in our own little pet idea, and before we realized it, God would look like our work and our idea, instead of our work looking like a reflection of the beautiful face of God. These things are God's way of keeping us in love with Himself—and keeping us from falling in love with someone else. . . . God can so easily and completely be left out of our love."

"But even I distrust myself. It's not just *them* thinking that maybe I am nuts, or overcompensating. I don't think it would bother me if it were just them. It's *me*. I wonder too. How do I know that He wants me to do these things —to go to church every morning, to say grace when no one else is bothering to say it, to shy away from some conversations? How do I know I'm not just being a prude—or worse?"

"If I think you are doing something you shouldn't, I'll stop you. Meanwhile, don't worry about being too sure. When we are too sure of ourselves, we grow proud, and pride takes us from God. These uncertainties keep us humble."

"Father, you make it sound so simple!" I sighed, doubtfully.

"Just be a little patient," he replied, "love ardently, and have faith. These things will pass."

"I certainly hope so."

Father Kirby laughed. "You are all right," he told me. "They will."

41. My Own Crazy Way

I HAD DONE my share of snickering at people who passed out religious leaflets or preached in the parks or streets: now one day I found myself on the boardwalk of a public beach passing out leaflets condemning racial discrimination as a sin against Christ and saying loudly, for all to hear, why we should be Christians. I had wanted to be a writer, rich and famous; now I didn't want to write at all, unless it could be something that would help others to find God and love Him. The ideas of penance and suffering had repelled me; now I wanted to share Our Lord's suffering and do penance for all who would not because they did not love Him, that they might be given grace to love Him too. I had believed that there was a middle plane, neither good nor evil, wherein men might live and walk securely; now I was certain that outside God was no life at all, and to walk without Him was to walk with death. I had believed that I could mind my own business while a whole world suffered, starved and died around me without speaking or acting in protest; now I knew that we are our brother's keepers.

Things had certainly changed, and beyond all reason, for grace transcends reason. So I was afraid. I thought I was crazy.

But all the time I saw the "sane" world around me going berserk, and sinking deeper and deeper into the mires of paganism and conflict. The greatest scientific discovery of the age was being used not to save but to destroy life. Billions of dollars were being spent to arm nations, while other nations died of slow starvation, while children froze to death, having no shelter, and while young girls sold their bodies for bread. New housing projects rose to relieve the critical housing shortage and provide good living conditions for families in low income groups, but these projects were closed to "undesirable races." "Undesirable races" were usually Negroes, but Jews and Orientals were sometimes excluded too.

Then I began to wonder if it were I who was crazy. One day I saw an essay by Peter Maurin, and I thought I had the answer. I quote it as I remember it:

"People say I am crazy. They say I am crazy because I refuse to be crazy the way everybody else is crazy. The way everybody else is crazy, I know I would be crazy. So I'll go on being crazy in my own crazy way, and I'm trying to make other people crazy my way."

Peter was right. All at once I knew I wanted to make people crazy his way too. When I made this decision, I think I began to clutch at the truth which will enable me to stand, that I might walk; the truth that admits God is not only our peace and salvation, but even our sanity. I was not crazy, nor were those others who spent their lives in praising God or in trying to make the world a Christian world for His glory. The secular world is not a sane society either. Sin and enslavement to sin are not sanity, nor are sensuality and enslavement to sensuality. The saint is opposed to all our sensual and materialistic ideals, because he is eminently sane. To seek sanctity, then, is to seek sanity; it is to seek to fulfill the laws and fill the needs of our whole selves in God.

My friend Emily, also a student nurse at the hospital, a Negro and an Episcopalian, with many ideals and ideas like my own, used to talk to me about this. She admired the work and workers at *The Catholic Worker*. She called us "Papists" but agreed that this "crazy way" is the hope of society, and so it became her way too though she never entered the Church. "We're working off our hostilities," she joked, in good psychiatric terms. But all the same, she was careful to go to frequent communion in her own church, and encouraged me in going to mine.

42. New Friends

I WAS VERY GLAD when I went to Kingston Avenue Hospital for my tuberculosis and contagious disease affiliation. There were about thirty in my class, representing about six different schools of nursing. Most of the other classes were about the same size. I was the only student from my school, and the only Negro student in the whole school, until the last month, when another colored student came with the group from Fordham Hospital. There must have been about twenty schools of nursing affiliated with the school, perhaps more.

When I first arrived, I wondered if the girls would like me, or if I would be able to make friends among the other students. Most of the students from my hospital told me that affiliating students kept within their own hospital group and were not very friendly with others. My friend and "big sister" (upper classman), Emily, told me not to worry about it, that I would find them friendly if I was. "They are judging by themselves," she said.

Once at Kingston Avenue, I could see how right she was. They were so different from the students at my hospital. They reminded me more of those at Harlem Hospital and Misericordia. They were friendly and natural, and when they talked their conversation was not limited to gossip and trivialities. Soon I made friends with some from Flower & Fifth Avenue, St. John's (Long

Island City), and Brooklyn Jewish. My best friends were from Brooklyn Jewish—Betty Shipiro, Charna, Janet and one whose name I have forgotten now, a girl from Canada.

We talked together about many things, our faiths, our ambitions, the race problem as it affected both our races, our hopes and desires, even our secret dreams. Sometimes we went to Janet's house or Betty's and those times were best of all. Sometimes we went swimming at Coney Island, or simply walking around the hospital neighborhood or shopping. Those were good times too.

At Betty's house we experimented with cooking for each other. The Jewish dishes were strange to me.

"A few more months and we will be finished," the Canadian girl would exult.

"Yes, it's been a long, hard course. I'm glad it's ending," Betty said. "There's so much I want to do when I'm through. Charna and I are going to travel. First we are going to California together."

"My 'little sister,' Adrian, from my hospital wants to travel too. She's going to Palestine. I'd like to go there, but I'll take care of Butch and have a handful," I declared. "What about you, Janet?"

"I'm still going to get married as soon as I can find me a fellow, and have a baby like yours. Gee, I bet you miss him. What's his daddy like?"

Betty saved my answering: "Helen doesn't talk about that," she said. "It's a wonder you wouldn't like to go over there too, to Palestine, to Jerusalem, you're so religious and all. Did you ever think that's where our faiths met? And there is one God, after all."

Another night we were talking in her room, just Betty

and I. Betty was trying to explain to me her attitude toward God and religion.

"I don't say I don't believe," she said. "But there are some things I don't see. At home, you know, we aren't very strict in keeping the old laws, but my mother believes a lot of it. I want to. But I look around, especially here in the hospital, and see so much suffering—needless, hopeless, and in those who are innocent and don't deserve it. Why? What can justify that, if God is just and merciful and loves us?"

I tried to show her something of the Christian concept of suffering as a means of grace, redemption. I pointed out the natural good that even she could see come from and through suffering. Then I tried to show her how we who are Christian believe that suffering can be a means of union with God and salvation for our fellows.

When I finished she said she understood but was not sure she agreed.

43. The Way of the Cross

THE NEXT DAY I was off duty except for classes, so I was in my own room when the floor maid told me I had a special delivery letter at the desk. I picked it up and brought it back to my room to read. It was from my mother. My son was in the hospital paralyzed from the waist down with polio.

My first impulse, after the pain and shock of the knowledge had subsided, was to go at once to my superintendent of nurses and ask leave to go to Memphis. Yet I knew that there was nothing I could do in Memphis but wait and pray, and she might easily point out that this I could do in New York. Apparently the crisis was over, he was in no danger unless there was some change, and none was expected. In three weeks I would be finished with my affiliation and would be going home anyway.

So I went instead to my nursing supervisor and explained the situation to her. She was very understanding and sympathetic and told me: "If there is any change, you can certainly go home if necessary." I thought of all I had told Betty the night before, and I know she did too, when I told her I prayed that I was accepting the suffering in the light of those words and that others or I might by it be drawn closer to God.

Weeks had never passed so slowly as those last at the

hospital, but at last the time for vacation came. I bought my ticket and packed my things, in order that I could leave as soon as I came off duty that day. I went on duty with a light heart and said goodbye to all my patients. I called my friend, Emily, who was going with me, and we made last minute plans. Everything was ready.

About ten o'clock, my supervisor called me. There was something so grave about her voice that, without knowing why, I was frightened. Something was wrong; I wondered if I had failed my examinations. It was with much trepidation that I went down to her office.

"Miss Caldwell," she said, "this is our medical director."

For the first time I noticed the man seated there and felt my knees grow weak. Student nurses are not called down to meet the medical director of a hospital for trifles.

He cleared his throat and began as gently as he could: "We looked at your X-ray and found something there . . ."

He was telling me that I had tuberculosis. I could not go home. I must go to the hospital.

I was sent to my own hospital, and the infirmary nurse went with me to a chest specialist affiliated with some of the city hospitals. He examined me and looked at my X-rays, then declared, "She's a definite case of tuberculosis, but not a compensation case."

I wanted to know what a "compensation case" was.

He explained. "Sometimes people get sick and want to say the city is responsible, so they can be paid while they are being treated for their illness. But you have had this disease ever since you entered the hospital as a student. So you aren't entitled to compensation."

I felt numbed and too weak to stand. I could not believe

that I had been ill for months while everyone had pretended I was well, or misread the monthly X-rays every time until now. And I would need money while I was taking the cure—but where was I going to get it?

When I returned to my bed in the hospital I was thoroughly miserable, wallowing in my misery, drowning myself in it without a struggle. My cross seemed too heavy to bear.

I don't know now how long I would have continued in this state, but just then the nurse brought me in a copy of the paper, *Camillus*. I read it and found in it a tale about a woman who, after one of those winters when every imaginable calamity seems to have occurred, said to Our Lord, "Lord, I know you won't send me more than I can bear, but I do wish you didn't have such a good opinion of me."

That made me laugh, and all was well again. Of course, I had a cross. It is the very symbol of Christianity. What I wanted was the grace to bear it patiently. I prayed for grace, for the help of God.

44. Recovery

I WAS IN THE SANITARIUM nineteen months taking the "cure." The time passed quickly, although at the beginning, it seemed like an eternity. My friends wrote regularly and sent me the things I wanted and needed. Every two weeks a priest came to hear our confessions and bring us Holy Communion. And of course God was always near, even when we were unaware of His Presence.

My son was almost completely well and could walk and run again. So it was a happy time, and I had many things for which to be thankful. If God had given me a cross, He had also given me Simons and Veronicas to go with me on the way.

It was a strange time, though, with many adjustments to be made. I had almost never shared a room with anyone, then suddenly I was sharing a room with ten or twelve people, day and night, strangers of different ages, races, likes and dislikes. Never before had I realized so well that privacy is a privilege, almost a luxury. Like health, I had always taken it for granted. And silence. Never had I realized how precious it can be.

In a ward, you eat, sleep, dress, read, laugh and cry while others look on. Often, if you want a place for recollection, like St. Catherine of Siena, you must seek it within your own soul. After a while you learn to pray or concentrate with two or three radios blaring, all tuned to different stations, and an argument going on around you full blast. You learn to accept the simple, painful annoyances that are part of your treatment and cure: things like rest hours that have to be observed four or five times a day, just when you would rather be doing something else, or pneumo-thorax treatments which have to be taken every week. There are disappointments and setbacks, and always the dreary slowness and monotony to try your faith and patience. Your friends and family now become letters, and there is a horrible empty feeling in you when you don't receive any. And all the while you feel so useless. You think you should be doing something for Our Lord instead of lying there like a rotten log. You almost wish you had some real pain, so you could offer it up for sinners. This seems like a mockery even of illness, because you don't even feel sick. At least, that's the way it was with me.

Yet it is just such simple daily annoyances as these that Our Lord expects us to bear patiently. It is these little, seemingly insignificant sacrifices and offerings that he requires of all. We aren't all called to live lives of heroic sanctity like St. Catherine of Siena or St. Rose of Lima. But we are called to be saints. And our sanctification consists in the cheerful and willing acceptance and offering of all that we are and have, small or great. No one can offer more. It is our love and the will to please Him that matter most to Our Lord.

I was in Otisville Sanitarium in Otisville, New York, three months and then was transferred to Stony Wold in the Adirondacks because it was supposed to be "better." "A lot of doctors and nurses go there," someone assured me, waving some beautiful pictures of the place under my nose. "There is a lot more privacy, and everything." So I went and it was there that I wrote most of this story.

There I made many friends, and I am sorry to say, a few enemies. Perhaps I am wrong about this, though. I hope so. But sometimes I use my tongue and my pen in a way other people don't like. There for a year I edited the "San" paper, the *Sez*. Sometimes I told inconvenient truths, and was in hot water more than once. At the end of fifteen months it was decided that I would be happier elsewhere, to no one's surprise. My friends and I had expected that for a long time and were ready for it.

The *Sez* spoke for the patients, for the good of all. Some patients felt that there was discrimination and favoritism shown against the "city" patients (those whose bills were paid by the City of New York, of whom I was one), and the patients whose families paid their bills, or whose expenses were taken care of through Workmen's Compensation. Many felt that there was racial discrimination, especially against Negroes, but also against the Jews, and felt this very keenly, like a pain.

Many felt that the attitudes of some of the nurses toward the patients left much to be desired. These and similar problems, added to those which came inevitably from simply being ill with a disease like tuberculosis and having to be away from family and friends with scarcely ever a visitor, seemed greatly unfair. In satire, in allegory and sometimes indirectly or directly in editorials, the *Sez* presented these problems and spoke for the silent.

Whether all of these problems were real, or some a combination of unfortunate coincidence and overwrought nerves and imagination, I do not know. I know many of the things changed or were modified afterwards to some extent after the *Sez* presented them. And I know no transfer ever came through so quickly as that for the editor of the *Sez*. They even bought the ticket, she being broke at the time, and helped her pack.

But that is getting ahead of the story. A lot of other things happened before that. For one thing, I made a final decision concerning myself and George. During all of this time I had continued to write to him, telling him of myself and Butch, but resolutely avoiding any references to our future together, making no promises, but saying, "Wait until you come home. We will discuss it then, when things are normal, and we both know what we want to do and what we can."

He kept saying for over a year that he would be discharged soon, but at last he really was. He telegraphed that he was coming up to see me, but he never did. There was no further word for about a month, while the police at the town from which he had sent the telegram searched for him at my request. I thought that something had happened to him. The chief was very kind and wanted to help but said he could find no trace beyond an uncle's house. He would keep me posted, though, he promised.

Then I had another letter. There was little explanation. The month might have been a day, and the promise of no account. It was as a child might have acted and written in such circumstances. But George was not a child and neither was I. And two years in the navy's detention barracks seemed to have done little or nothing for his sense of responsibility. As far as I could see, he was not essentially different from the spoiled, irresponsible boy I had left almost three years before. Then I had believed that he was not the kind of father that would help me to build a Christian home for our son, now I believed it still more firmly. I knew—too well—what life in an unhappy, divided, or broken home was like. I did not want that for my son. I felt that I would rather he should not know his father at all than that he should know him to his sorrow. And we were not even making a good beginning.

His interests were not mine, but I thought we could overleap that. His plans and hopes for the future were not for the things for which I would plan or hope, but I believed that we could compromise on that. His faith was not mine—in fact, as far as I could see, he had no faith—but I even hoped that we could go beyond that. But now it had become clear that he wasn't even an adult, he was not responsible or dependable. There was nothing I could do about that, and it was no use trying to fool myself. So I told him not to write any more and refused to write or to answer his letters.

He said that I was being unfair and spiteful. He reminded me that Butch needed a father. I began to question my decision; maybe I was just angry, "cutting off my nose to spite my face." I talked it over with my confessor. I told him the whole story from beginning to end, leaving nothing out, exonerating myself in nothing. He listened silently and patiently until I had finished.

"It is hard," he said at last, "but I think you have made the right decision."

"But do you think I have any duty to him now?"

"Under the circumstances, I think not, except to that extent that every Christian has a duty to his fellows. Pray for him and be at peace."

So I let my decision stand and I didn't worry about it. I have not been sorry.

Another thing that happened was that I began to write in earnest. Another patient, Grace Peluso, typed the shorter things for me. When an editor accepted a manuscript, we celebrated with ice cream or soda. When he didn't, we tried again.

Grace and I did a lot of other things together, too. She was Italian, a Catholic and very pretty. She loved the Church, and we talked together of her and her Divine Founder. We said our prayers together—the *Little Office of the Blessed Virgin Mary* and the Rosary. Sometimes we made holy hours together, but twice we got into trouble for this. Once because it was night and we should have been in bed, and once because the nurse thought we should have been somewhere else. We played together with others in our dormitory—word games, cards or Chinese checkers.

In fact, the whole group in the dorm was a very congenial one for the first year. Nine of us came up together and were put in the same room, one of the few dormitories, or porches. (Most of the "San" was made up of semi-private rooms.) We had arguments and discussions which lasted later into the night than we were supposed to talk, but they were without heat or bitterness. There were five white, all Northerners, including one fair Porto Rican (because I think she was considered white there). They were Italian, Bohemian and Jewish. There were four Negroes, including two from the South, one New Yorker and one West Indian. We were Methodist, Baptist, Seventh Day Adventist, Catholic and Jewish. That gave us a lot to talk about. We talked about our religions, the racial problem, the South, the West Indies, Porto Rico, marriage, our sickness, our plans for the future, all the things a mixed group like that can think of in a year of sharing the same rooms, many of the same problems and sufferings, the same disappointments, the same fears. On Sundays and some other days we sang together—Negro spirituals, hymns or folk songs. In the mornings we read, wove, crocheted or knitted; those who knew how to do these things already, patiently taught those who did not. Some embroidered or sewed by hand. We made sweaters, afghans, dresses, many types of handwork for families and friends.

In the afternoon, after the mid-day rest period, we played games. At night we talked. Once four of us gave a surprise play for the others. They didn't know what we planned until the day we presented it. That was not as hard to accomplish as it might seem. When did we practice? The four of us—Ann, Grace, Gloria and I—were all Catholics. At that time we were in the habit of saying the *Little Office* together. Later, we had to stop, at the request of one member of the hospital staff. It seemed that we were disturbing the tray boys, floor sweeper, hospital attendants, or some such persons who had noticed us while they worked. We never quite knew the source of the complaint, since we were blissfully unaware of creating any disturbance. But at the time I am speaking of, our room mates were used to seeing us go out to the solarium, and they never interrupted us. We were practicing while they thought we were still saying our prayers. So the play, a comedy, was a success; everyone enjoyed it.

In all our playing, working, or living together we never had an argument that we couldn't settle among ourselves that first year. Once Ann was angry at me, and once Grace was, and there were a few similar situations between some others. But we kept it among ourselves, and after a while it passed. That was very different from the relations between other groups in the San. Maybe our isolation was partly responsible. The building was so constructed that except for one private room, for many months empty, then occupied by a Negro doctor who was recovering and who later joined the staff, we were alone on the floor. Under us was the Infirmary. There the rules were stricter, because the patients were still very ill. And we didn't visit them very often.

After the first year there were changes. A lot of new patients were admitted, and some to our dorm. Others from our dorm were moved to another building where the routine was the same as ours, to Upper and Lower Alley. The patients moved from our dorm were all white at first, and those who moved in, all colored. While there were still empty beds in the infirmary, a colored patient on strict bed rest—the kind of patient usually admitted to the infirmary—was sent to Lower Alley, and one colored patient was transferred there to be her room mate. The new patient complained of the noise—most of those patients were getting well and acted as if they were well —and asked to be transferred to the infirmary. The nurse suggested that she put cotton in her ears. As the patient was herself a registered nurse and accustomed to the courtesies of the profession, she felt this very keenly. At the same time the patients began to say among themselves that ours was a Negro ward. Patients began predicting what ward another patient would be moved to before they were moved, or before they were admitted on the basis of race. Each time they were right.

When we first heard what others were saying about our dorm, we were angry and incredulous. But when the guesses proved so consistently correct, we began to have our own doubts. When, one day, two new beds were made in our dorm, everyone said the patients would be colored. We hoped that they were wrong. We insisted that they could be. We didn't like to be referred to as "the Jim Crow ward."

The new patients were white. They came in and made themselves comfortable in bed. They remained perhaps thirty minutes, not longer, and were transferred to another ward.

Later a nurse came up and volunteered the information that the two patients had small babies at home and were lonely, and wanted to be moved where they could see the lake. We knew that one could get an excellent view of the lake by simply walking across the room through one short hall to the solarium, and when we thought of our own long months of loneliness and our friends' and our own small babies at home; when we thought of their requests for transfers and some of our own, for much better reasons than that, and how they had been refused, the words sounded wholly forced and unbelievable. It seemed to most of us that the patients in Upper and Lower Alley had been right.

All but Louise. She was from Brooklyn, and somehow had never come in contact with racial prejudice, and she did not believe it existed, not at Stony Wold and not in the South, and not anywhere here in our country. She believed that we imagined all of these things. She was angry at all of us, but especially at Grace, because of the things we said we believed. She put her anger into words and said she did not want to stay in the same ward with us any more. So she was moved. At last we had found a problem that we could not settle quietly among ourselves. The whole San knew and talked.

The *Sez* spoke of things like this in general but not as reporting news, because there was no proof. Besides this, it had to pass censorship before it appeared, and if direct accusations had been made, they would never have been allowed in the paper. Not that my censor, a Southerner, was prejudiced herself. I am convinced, as were most, that if racial, religious or class prejudice existed there, she had no part in it, she did not approve it. In fact, if it did exist, it was only in a few, but, unfortunately for us, a powerful few.

I have already said what happened when the *Sez* continued writing these things.

45. Return

AT SEAVIEW on Staten Island, where I was sent,
I was discharged in a week, an "apparently arrested"
case, to the outpatient department for pneumo-thorax
refills. In another week, I was on my way home to
Memphis. My friend Emily paid part of my fare and
went with me to the train. Before I left, I stopped to see
my friends at the *Catholic Worker* who had been so kind
to me during the many months of illness. I wanted to go
to St. Michael's to see my friends there, but there wasn't
time, so I said farewell to New York for awhile.

In Memphis, the whole family met me at the station—
Don, Mother, Lawrence and Butch. "That's my mother,"
Butch announced happily. "Mother, was you in the
hospital resting and you came home on the choo-choo
train?"

So that was a glad homecoming. Sunday, Mother and
I went to church together. She had also been received
into the Church during my absence, and it was a joy to
go to the altar with her to receive the Body of Our Lord.

The next week I took the children (son and nephew)
to Holly Springs to see Daddy. That was another glad
homecoming. The only thing that spoiled it a little was
something he couldn't help. I couldn't go to Mass because
there was no priest for the colored chapel that week.
Things had changed since I had been away. White and

Negro no longer went together. When I went to the "white" church, Father Paul explained to me very kindly that this was St. Joseph's parish and that Negroes did not attend services there, not even the Mass. *St. Joseph's* parish! (St. Joseph, Patron of the Universal Church, pray for us!) He explained that there would be devotions at the colored church as soon as he had said his Mass. He gave me Holy Communion and promised to come to my house and get me later and take me to the other church for devotions. And I went home.

That is a terrible, ugly thing, isn't it? You who love the Church and see in her Christ's Mystical Body will tremble. You who hate her, if any of you have read this far, will be glad. You who are still smug, complacent, or indifferent about your faith and your Church, might wake up a bit more to your place in her and duties to her. But none of us must allow ourselves to see in this action of one priest, the Church. It is not consistent with what she has taught and practiced through the ages. It does not agree with what the Popes have said. Nor can we even judge the priest himself, only his action. And that we must forgive. Even if it had been thought out and intended as an act of racial hate, we would have to forgive it, since Our Lord has forgiven all of us much more than that. But I do not believe it was that.

Nothing Father Paul has ever done or said (including that action) has ever given me reason to believe that he was, or is, himself prejudiced. He is in a peculiar situation, and did what he thought best at the time. I do not think it was best. Perhaps after he had thought it over, he did not think so either, because at a later visit one week day, when there was no Mass at the chapel for the colored, he did take me with the sisters to the church for the white to hear Mass. But at that time, he explained to me that they were having a lot of trouble getting white converts, and some of the townspeople were very bitter because of their (Father Paul's and the Sisters') attention to Negro welfare. They had built a school for Negroes, though there was no Catholic school for whites, and they were trying to make it a success. Now they needed white friendship and help—especially since there were no Negro Catholics in the town, or Negroes interested in the Church who could help. There was a lot of opposition to what he was trying to do, particularly from a certain Baptist minister, who had spoken against him from the pulpit. He was trying to help the Negro and keep down racial friction at the same time by showing the townsmen that he was not trying to make the Negro forget his "place," nor advocating "social equality," a term most hated in the South. He was being "prudent."

The only thing he forgot was that that kind of prudence has no place in the Mystical Body of Christ, in the life of the Church. He forgot that the Church is *One*, Holy and Universal, and that the Mass is for all, so that no baptized person can lawfully be forbidden to hear and offer it, to satisfy the prejudices of a few, or of a majority.

I went with him to the chapel for the devotions. There was Benediction of the Blessed Sacrament. As I looked at the Host, I wept. It would seem that His crucifixion was still not over. Some of His lesser members must still be nailed to His cross. That hurt very much. I tried not to think of it any more, except to pray for the blindness of people to the law of God and the greatness of man.

46. "Pre-Catholic" Action

AFTER I WENT BACK to Memphis, I wrote to several of my friends, telling them I had arrived safely, and about my trip. I also told some of the incident in Holly Springs. Among these were my friends at the *Catholic Worker*. Dorothy wrote back and asked if she could print the letter in the *Worker*, and I replied in the affirmative.

In the meantime, while I was at home resting, I wanted something to do. Since I was writing anyway, a friend suggested I write for our local colored paper, *The Memphis World*. I sent in a few articles to the editor and he liked them, so I began a regular column for the paper and called it "Looking Things Over."

Shortly after the *Worker* came out the next month, with my letter in it, I came out of church one morning to find two young white boys waiting for me. Both had seen my letter, and it was a simple matter to find out which parish I belonged to in the city. One was William Curry, the other Jack Kelly. They were interested in starting an interracial Catholic Action or discussion group, and was I? Of course I was, so we talked. That first day, we compared notes, so to speak, and made plans. We didn't know anyone who would be interested in the project so far but ourselves. Bill knew one girl who might, and promised to bring her to meet me. I knew one boy who would probably be, but in a few weeks he would be going off to college. But we decided to try, anyway.

That night Bill brought Margie over, and we talked. We talked of the *C. W.* and Catholic Action mostly. In the end, we had decided on a method of procedure. We had decided also how we could get members.

I wrote to Dorothy and asked for the names and addresses of Memphis subscribers. These, we knew, would understand what we were trying to do, and might be sympathetic. Bob sent me the names and addresses, and we found the telephone numbers. We got in touch with each one (even tried to reach two who were dead because we didn't know they were).

One or two were not interested. About the same number pleaded "too busy." But most agreed to come at least to the first meeting. They, in turn, also gave us names of others who might be interested, and we got in touch with them.

At the first meeting there were about twenty-five, maybe one or two more or less. There was a lot of misunderstanding to be cleared up there. Some imagined it was to be chiefly an interracial action group conducted by Catholics. Some thought it was to be a Catholic Action cell. Some thought it was to be a militant Catholic Action group. We insisted that the group was to be interracial, but not directed primarily toward the racial problem, only indirectly, as a part of our group life together or Christian actions apart. We pointed out that we were not ready for any but very limited action now, because we had too much to learn; this was to be, at least at first, a study group. We would have to learn the truths of our faith before we could teach them to others;

and live and practice them habitually, or at least regularly and fervently, before we could communicate them to others. We would have to know what would be a good temporal order before we could start criticizing the one we have—at least, before such criticism could mean anything in fruitfulness. We would have to have advice and counsel from a representative of the Church to keep us headed in the right direction.

A few were all for immediate action, any kind of action, just so that it was action; they were tired of talk. A few had come because they were curious. These never came back.

But from week to week the group grew. Some dropped out and new ones came. By November we had a steady group of about fifteen who came regularly, and we had four interested who were away in schools, two Negro and two white. We had (and have) professional people and workers, married men and women and single ones. There were (and are) housewives, nurses, teachers, and students, Negro and white. Over a cup of coffee and cookies, or the equivalent, we exchange ideas on our problems, and we study. We started with the Encyclical on the Mystical Body. Now we have begun on the Liturgy.

Usually we meet at the rectory of the priest who was kind enough to encourage and help us. Sometimes we have parties and meet at the home of one or the other member of the group. We pay no dues, we have no officers, and the majority does not necessarily rule. We are trying to learn to recognize and to follow leadership. Sometimes we have Communion Breakfast together. Except for that, and simply being together as an interracial group in the heart of the South, we have not tried to branch out into any action yet, except once. That was when we decided to gather clothes for the children of the Catholic school in Holly Springs because they are very poor. Sister Eustelle there, who received them very gladly, has promised us all the action we need this Spring, however, if, she says, by "action" we mean work. There are desks to be sandpapered, and painting to be done, and lots of other things like that. She has invited us to share the work and to have a picnic there if we wish, and we probably will. Meanwhile we are studying and praying together for grace for ourselves and for our peoples, that all may learn to love each other as we are learning to love each other, that we may better ourselves and the society in which we live, and make Christ's kingdom come on earth, even as He taught us to pray. Of course, we are very little people for such a big job—but didn't Christ say He loved the little ones and would bless them? It is this that gives us hope.

47. We Are All One

Sooner or later we all get a push, so that we
must choose one side of the fence or the other: God or
the world.

Looking at this choice superficially, we seem to see on
the world's side, success, fame, security, progress and
unlimited freedom to find pleasure where we may without the need to consider "abstract" ideas of good and
evil. We see only convenience and expediency and all
those goods which our modern education has taught us
to value so highly.

Whereas on God's side, we seem to see suffering, ridi-
cule, failure, reaction, unwanted responsibility to love
and serve God and men, and to obey even when obedience is not expedient—all those things that make up the
narrow "way of the cross."

Viewed in this light it does seem as if those things of
the world are the things men most want. If this were true,
then the Negro doesn't have a chance. Neither does God
—or so it would seem.

But we must not see superficially. We must look be-
neath the surface. Then we see a furious racing for
progress—but toward what? We see increased freedom—
to do what? We see pleasures that end with their own
satisfaction, and every gain another man's loss. We see
a longer life—but for what?

We conquer the atom, the sun and the stars. We increase the human life-span years—but then what? In the end death is the victor and we have to come back to God anyway—and with an emptiness that even He can't fill.

But on God's side, the picture is different. We see a constant reaching upward toward a definite goal higher than the universe itself. We hear a constant strain of joyful praise in and through the suffering. Failure becomes success, and death is victory. In poverty we are richest, and each man's gain is every man's gain, for God is in all and all in God, and all are filled with the fullness of God.

Viewed in this, the true light, it becomes obvious that the Negro does have a chance, equal to all, to reach the highest goal possible to men: sanctity, and to possess the greatest Good of all: God.

And as for God's chances, I'll bet on Him any time.

"For you are all the children of God through faith in Christ Jesus. For all you who have been baptized into Christ, have put on Christ. There is neither Jew nor Greek; there is neither slave nor freeman; there is neither male nor female. For you are all one in Christ Jesus."

Date Due